Gateways 2 Peace

Gateways 2 Peace

Polly Wirum

Columbus, Ohio

Gateways 2 Peace

Published by Gatekeeper Press
2167 Stringtown Rd, Suite 109
Columbus, OH 43123-2989
www.GatekeeperPress.com

Copyright © 2018 by Polly Wirum

All rights reserved. Neither this book, nor any parts within it may be sold or reproduced in any form or by any electronic or mechanical means, including information storage and retrieval systems without permission in writing from the author. The only exception is by a reviewer, who may quote short excerpts in a review.

ISBN (paperback): 9781642371628
eISBN: 9781642371635

Printed in the United States of America

Table of Contents

Part I: Developing Awareness ix
Where do you put your awareness? 1
The Rattlesnake in the Wine Bottle 5
Making Happiness Stick 9
It"s Time to Connect to the Higher Vibrations! 15
Defining Balance 17
The Process of Healing 23
Finding the Miracle in Death 27
The Importance of Hope 35
Past Travels 39
Part II: Processes 43
What's Your Fear Factor? 45
Dial in the frequency of Love 51
A Clear Mind 55
The Universal Truth Is the Absence of Doubt 59
The Sound of Vibrational Change 65
Sensitivity is beautiful! 69
Call to Mind 73
Empowered 77
New Beginnings 81
Part III: Results 87

The Vibration of Peace 89
Winning 91
Super charged Energy 95
Our Consciousness is Everything 99
Circle of Divinity 103
Expanding through Karma 107
We See through the Same Eyes 111
Healing from The Inside Out 121
Touching Clarity 125
Spiritual Wellness 131
Abundance and Everything 135
Enjoy The Moment 139
The Brilliance of Love 143

Part I: Developing Awareness

Where do you put your awareness?

HELLO! I HOPE this moment finds you in a place of wellness and ease. And if it doesn't... maybe some of these words will shine a light on your personal path to wellness.

I have just returned from an amazing time in Carmel Valley, California with my husband. The hiking was heavenly. My days were filled with ridges of grass and trees as far as I could see. The community was made up of horses and dogs. The ocean was near. I was given time to bask in what makes me happy! This is something I know is vital to each of us. I wish it for you.

What is it that brings you to that place of open heart and appreciation? A place where time is not a commodity? A place where you fully experience the moment?

Having a daily practice of meditation or prayer and a sense of community is important to our wellness. We also need to find experiences for our senses that remind us of our physical body on Earth… AND our connection to something so much greater, our ability to create heaven on earth. This sounds almost too good to be true. Is it possible to feel so good on earth when we see the potential for suffering?

What if we only opened our eyes to a day filled with joy?

What if we opened our heart to only experience love? What if we only heard sounds that made us feel good? Now you're getting it. We literally have unlimited possibilities to choose from while creating life. Bring in the joy. Allow yourself to create a world so good it feels like fiction. Why not? We are literally experiencing what we think is the correct version. Living a life that is filled with stress, anger, illness and confusion is just as fictional.

Imagine you have multiple worlds that are all available to you. One is filled with the energy of love ones, including those who have passed. It's also filled with guidance and abundance. It's overflowing with a feeling of completion. It's the world where you thrive and share your most creative version of yourself. Miracles are manifested here.

Another world contains the ideas of lack, fear, and limited time. Many of us combine these two possible world experiences. But what if you decide you're ready for the shift to living in joy? The shift to expanded conscious? It's up to each of us to decide how we experience life. And what we summon into our life.

The above message is just a stepping stone in understanding the reality you call life. It's important to remember we each choose our life experiences or reality. Much of what you're experiencing was chosen by you long ago.

How can it be long ago, you might ask? When there is no sequence of time…

There are parallel universes that shift and even blend into each other. You are the same energy in one, as in the others. Where do you want your awareness to take hold? Are you seeking the awareness of all? Or are you living in an incomplete vision that limits your senses and ability to perceive?

You can transform the here and now by awakening all your abilities to perceive this higher power in yourself. Each experience that brings you closer to joy, closer to our creator, is the path to experiencing your expanded awareness.

You personally choose to have this variety of experiences believing it would complete the karmic cycle… There is not so much a cycle, as there is an unlimited amount of life choices. It has all happened already. Whatever you can dream of exists in the here and now. We are only now stepping in to help you understand each individual's power to choose their own life experiences.

Imagine the different realities or levels of consciousness or awareness all interacting with each other. Imagine that your soul is taking part and experiencing reality on each level. Some are at a higher vibrational level then others… much like the shape of a pyramid. This is the interesting part. You get to choose at what level you're working on, or recognizing as reality. In other words, you get to choose your life experiences.

Remember, it is all happening now. Every moment is now. Everything is a possibility.

Helping others with this concept raises the overall vibration level. There is a period of readjustment. Understand that the soul of you in another world is the same soul in this world. It only takes connecting with the world you want to truly experience. All lives add up to one or create the whole. Where do you want your attention to reside? What feels good?

These are the words that allow you experience another reality. Where do you put your attention?

What do you want to be experiencing? Where is your attention taking you?

This change doesn't need to take place in a step-by-step process. For example, if someone wants to live part time in Hawaii, you might think that you first need to find the Hawaii home, buy it, etc. I believe we can shift our awareness to already experience the home in Hawaii… But if it makes it easier for the transition to this reality, take it step by step…

Tessa Rampersad - Unsplash

The Rattlesnake in the Wine Bottle

WHEN I was about nine years old, I was at a party on the Eel River. This was in a small rural community in Southern Humboldt California. The gathering was basically a party for adults. To this day, I'm not sure how I even got there.

The memorable aspect of this event was a rattlesnake in a wine bottle, that I proudly carried around. I remember someone had put a young rattlesnake in a short, round wine bottle. I thought this was the coolest thing. I ran all over the river rocks and sand with the wine bottle and rattlesnake.

I can't remember what happened to the rattlesnake or the wine bottle. As an adult I see many things wrong with a kid wandering around a river with a captive rattlesnake. At the time it was all a great adventure.

In my life I have been blessed with many interesting

experiences. Some of these were good choices and others not so much. Ultimately, every decision I committed to opened a door to a memorable life experience.

Luckily the rattle snake adventure did not end poorly. I shut that possibility down when I parted ways with the snake.

I was raised on a small farm. It was here that I was introduced to the companionship of all animals. It was also where I learned how to sit still outdoors and just feel. In the stillness, a door opened to a life that remembered the connection to animals and the energy of the Earth.

I distinctly remember a time when I was milking a cow by hand. It had been raining. My forehead was resting on her warm, wet flank. Life was good and uncomplicated.

Each of us have carried our version of a rattlesnake around, just as each of us have experienced telling moments of peace. We can find both rattlesnakes and harmony in our families and communities. In this moment, we are gifted with the ability to decide how we want to move through life. What is important to you?

My life experiences brought me to live as a vegan. This was a direct link to my childhood. It is also a lifestyle reinforced through my personal spiritual beliefs. I encourage you to look at the many paths you've traveled. Is there anything you're willing to close the door on? Is there anything that you would like to commit yourself to in a deeper way?

Let me be guided by love and the lightness that allows me to find peace in every landscape. I am lifted free from worries that have bound me. I am free to explore all possibilities, however and whenever they appear in my vision. I am guided by love to the extent that I know only peace and joy in my heart. I greet you at this moment with the divine kinship we have created and share together. We together have created a matrix of undeniable miracles that shine down upon earth and radiate back to heavens above, the light and joy that we each carry inside.

We are each aware of the matrix of light energy. We each release our fears and allow this complex design within to birth the creator within. We have discovered a million ways to cover our brightness. Let us discover all the ways to share our brightness. Together let us not forget what we are created of, what we are made of – love, light, the purest form of communication with our souls. Shine the link to our creator which we are designed in the image of.

We wish you peace and ease as you discover the link to your ancestry down to the creator that rests within. Rest in the knowledge that we are designed by love for love. We guide you as one to the light within.

End of channel

I am learning more about our connection to source with my channeling. My understanding at this point is that we each have what is similar to a matrix of energy that we work with. Each matrix contains all possibilities, all lives, all time. Each of these matrixes are part of a bigger system, or source. We can imagine that these systems are really us in completeness.

Making Happiness Stick

We all experience good days and not so good days. Is it possible to increase the number of our good days as we continue to evolve? I know it is. In fact, I think that's the goal.

We all are created with energy and interact with energy. We have layers of energy within us and all around us. This energy is malleable and constantly changing. Energy rises to a higher vibration as we evolve. Energy also loves to find similar energy to interact with. The complex layers of our accumulated energy pulls to us the same energy as our thoughts and feeling. Some of what we attract is from today's thoughts and behaviors. Other attractions are from long ago, even lifetimes and generations ago.

Many of our hard-to-shake habits and beliefs are from lifetimes of subconsciously putting focus on certain beliefs. Each belief, chosen word, and action carries its own energy or combination of energy.

Imagine the energies that we have attracted are like colored thread woven through your DNA. Together they have organized the individual views you have during this life experience. We each tirelessly add more threads to our subconscious that are eventually displayed in our beliefs, habits, future and the future of our children.

How can we remove what doesn't serve us?

Start by writing down your frequently-used words. Next assign colors to your words. Choose colors that share the same energy as the words. This is completely personal. There is no right or wrong answer. Put these colors and words down on a big piece of paper. Give yourself enough room to really connect to this project. How do you feel when looking at your frequent words and thoughts in visual form? This is a great way to get a glimpse of the energy you're pulling into your world. It's also a great opportunity to identify what energy, colors, words and beliefs you want to be free of. You can record yourself in a conversation to see what words pop up the most. It might surprise you.

I'll give you some examples of a few of my words and thoughts and how I assigned them a color.

- How I feel when I'm listening to good music. I visualize lots of pink, orange, white, I see lots of moving colors. The colors I associate with my feelings depends on the music I'm listening to.

- How I feel when I see that my children are happy and successful… I feel strong, happy and satisfied. I associate this feeling with red, purple and indigo colors that shift in deliberate ways.

- How I feel when I'm outside in nature with the sun shining. I feel connected to everything! I see light yellow, white, orange. I associate lots of movement within the colors.

- How I feel when I think about the needless suffering and abuse that occurs. I recognize my energy decreases. I pull inward and I'm not as open to receive. I see cloudy, murky green and grey.

Notice that with my happy thoughts I saw lots of movement within my colors. On my example of feeling not so good, I noted a decreased flow of energy and I was not open to exchanging energy.

I believe we have the opportunity to make changes in our belief systems that change the past, present and future. They are all happening now. If we change our energy and what we attract, we change our world. We can change our experience and our world view.

There are many books and articles written on how to be happy. It's time to get happy. Pick the color or colors that remind you of happy. These colors should make you feel free, comfortable and at complete harmony with your surroundings. When you fully experience happiness, you're not allowing yourself to get tripped up in the colors or strings that drag you down. Just sit with the energy of happy and connect with all your colors of happy. Close your eyes and see your colors. I'm making this sound easy; over time it will be.

At this point visualize removing one unpleasant string of color at a time from your subconscious. As you gently remove this string and any string that resembles this color, pull it completely out and release it. Watch it transform into light. Fill the void where the ugly string was with your beautiful colors of happy. This is an exercise that can be done frequently. It's also an exercise that brings immediate results, and over time can bring lasting results. You can also incorporate breathing exercises when removing the unwanted strings.

It's also possible to use this practice to remove a belief that you hold on to. If a person doubts they are worthy of a good partner, their subconscious belief makes them feel and act a certain way. First, they need to examine how they feel and assign colors to the feelings. Next, they can start removing the colors associated with the belief, from their subconscious. The next step is to consciously change the words they use to describe themselves in relation to a partner. They will fill the void created by removing the negative, with beautiful colors of love and mantras of love.

You can also fill your rooms with the colors you associate with happiness. Display photos of your happy place. Change your environment to happy.

There's another possibility to help free yourself of the energy that is blocking your happiness: hypnosis. I've seen hypnosis create energy shifts in just one session. A skilled hypnotherapist is essentially a healer and an energy worker. They are able to pull lifetimes of threads and beliefs from your subconscious in just a few sessions.

I think hypnotherapy, along with healthy habits of meditation, prayer and other self-care habits, are wonderful tools for making happiness stick. If you're interested in hypnotherapy, do your research and find a certified, established hypnotherapist. Word of mouth is a great way to find someone not just good but great!

Let me know what you think about this exercise. It can be adapted for use with individuals that are not as visual.

Channeled message

The very beautiful life form that you are held in is stunning and magical and capable of so many gifts and moments of awareness. To fortify your human self, we ask you to remember what magnificence you're created from and connected to. Open your heart to the very wonders that pour through you. Bask in the love and guidance that we offer you. Breath in your awareness. Let the energy shift inside so you're aware of what you carry with in. It truly is an undiscovered world. We're so excited to teach you how to effortlessly connect to your unique spiritual formation. It's as easy as saying yes and inviting us into your world as we bring you into our shared world. Rest in the divine knowledge of peace that runs through you and I both at equal measures.

End of Channel

In this channel I discovered how the energy of our guides and angels and all divine energy melds into our energy. I would describe it as contact with those acting as our personal guides. Their energy melds into ours bringing us more aware of the Divine Energy. Thus vibrations are raised.

I have faith that we are merging into an awareness that will allow global shifts of love, compassion and peace. Together we are waking up.

It's Time to Connect to the Higher Vibrations!

YESTERDAY I WAS busy with appointments followed by family activities. I was in my **get things done** mode. While running errands I stopped by a kiosk to get a hot drink. When I purchased mine, I paid for another customer. This simple act totally changed my mood. The lovely customer was so surprised. She literally almost cried and said it was the nicest thing anybody has done for her in a long time.

It was such a great reminder that one of the easiest ways to raise your energy is to practice kindness. So, I encourage us all to practice random acts of kindness!

One of the really nice things about this moment is how it's easier than ever to connect with higher vibrations. I feel like the higher vibration energy source is somehow being made more readily available to us. This is wonderful news! It allows us to manifest easier. It allows us to connect with our Angels and guides easier. It also gives us more clarity and just helps us feel better.

So how are you going to make the connection? Easy. Random acts of kindness, prayer, meditation, laughter and faith! It's everything that you have heard or read before, but it will be easier to see the results! Go ahead and create the life you love!

I also wanted to share one other message. I see that President Donald Trump will not be able to fulfill his full term. It's unclear how it ends other than I see his energy leaving much like a deflated balloon. It could be as far in future as the 2nd or third year. Do watch for a health-related issue on the left side of his neck… And something with him losing his vision. The vision aspect could possibly be taken non-literally.

Rochelle Nicole - Unsp

Defining Balance

My intention to share experiences of healing has brought an abundance of changes into my world. One of them is for me personally!

In 2011, I ran my last marathon. I had not been feeling well for some time. It was the beginning of a significant life change for me. I truly loved to run, including marathons and other races. It was part of my lifestyle and identity. It made me feel strong and also provided me something to focus on besides family. Running gave me a sense of freedom. I even dreamed of running. I experienced

exhilaration and joy. Eventually running led me to a point of needed change. I reluctantly exchanged my passion for running with something else.

Struggling to get answers regarding my health, I waited and waited (not a comfortable experience for someone who likes things to move quickly). After almost a year of medical tests, I was finally diagnosed with a circulatory issue. It was a time of great frustration. To be honest, I still hold on to some of the issues with the medical care I received. I found myself having to let go of everything in my life, and to have faith that I would live to raise my children. My ability to live with faith is what brought me to my current life experience. I truly believe if we're not listening to our messages and ignore the signs that we're given, we will be stopped in our tracks. I went from working out almost daily to resting every day! I felt too tired and crappy to do much more.

I had been ignoring my intuitive abilities for years. It was during my many hours of daily resting that I found myself slipping into meditation. This was not planned. I also found myself praying again. It was not prayers just for myself and my family, but prayers for humanity. I found myself living again. I was using practices from my earlier years. I was back on track.

I have always believed in a higher power. I just wasn't putting my attention towards this connection. I was gifted with an awakening that affected all my mind, body and soul. Many names could be given to this experience; born again, Kundalini awakening, Spiritual Emergence. Whatever it's called, I was changed. I believe even on a cellular level.

It was over a couple of years that I gained increased awareness. The connection had always been there. I was just ignoring it. One day I will share some of the funny things that happened as I was adjusting to the new me. I'll also share how I started channeling messages.

But for today I'll get back to my love of running. In my mind, I had traded running for my awareness or spiritual connection. I accepted my body, mind and spirit were different. I didn't feel good when working out. This brought frustration and weight gain. For years I thought I could not attain the balance of being athletic and living intuitively. Eventually I was able to hike again, but running was still a past experience.

About six months ago I noticed I was feeling better. I could easily walk a half marathon. It was kind of exciting. This feeling kept growing. In July I went on a long hike with my family and was able to run a couple miles on the way out. I'm able to run today.

My current running is completely different from before. It connects me to the feeling of exhilaration I dreamed of before. I'm working out and feeling amazing! I still have my spiritual awareness and intuitive skills. I have just been allowed to appreciate my physical self on a new magnitude.

I wish you healing on whatever level you desire.

Channeled message

Enjoy the freedom of letting go. Feel our pull, our energy that guides you to brighter places. Tap into that core energy source. Imagine that you are weightless except for the connection to source. Feel the pull in your diaphragm. Your mind is free, your body is free. Imagine the ability to drift and ride the currents.

These currents are the prayers of all that have come and gone beyond you. These currents that you ride are the thoughts and prayers that are creating the expanded form of the human consciousness. There is so much to be grateful for. We're emerging and bringing in higher energy into the world for this miraculous occasion of transforming this moment into pure light energy. Imagine shifting back and forth between physical energy and light energy. What can you do with this? Where are you most comfortable? Both experiences have merit in the growth of your soul experience. We hold the circle of light all around you as you transform into your highest self. The transformation began with every moment, every thought, every prayer, every experience. You are not complete in only one form, for now. Experience all your heart desires. There is so much for you to explore. We're saving the best for last.

Imagining is allowing yourself transformation. When we ask you to imagine, it is us asking you, to allow yourself to be in a different level or different energy that is full of expansion. Imagine being lifted to such greater heights. This is your awareness or comprehension of all that exists. The shift of awareness has essentially already occurred.

You dance on the embers of what was left from the state of confusion that some exist in, but you have expanded and outlived the confusion. even in physical state you can shift to awareness and live in the light. Celebrate your choice of continuous living…

We're always with you   always with you   always with you

We are guiding you and stabilizing you in this time of energetic pulls and energy exchanges.

End of Channel

My understanding of this channel is that we truly are in a time of profound change. Those of us in physical form are here for a reason. Our ability to connect to the light and bring it to our Earth is a very powerful form of expansive energy for mankind. I believe we're here to help change our world with the power of love and light. And so it is.

Noah Silliman - Unsplash

The Process of Healing

In my thirties I went through a divorce and moved to Alaska. I had two very young children with me. As I began figuring out how I wanted to rebuild my life, I also examined my body. After having two children and breast-feeding for years, I was still fit and healthy. But when I looked at my breasts, I felt grief. It was shocking to me what had taken place over a short few years. Truthfully, I hated looking at my breasts in the mirror. Ouch… A vulnerable but truthful statement. I decided to get breast implants. Would I do it again? Very unlikely. At the time, it was part of a healing for my self-image.

I can't say I regret getting the implants. I will say, I never felt completely comfortable with them. I also thought of the maintenance factor if ever the saline bags ruptured. I decided to have them removed this Summer. I found a great doctor, picked the date and out the implants came, with a little lift! I also had scar tissue built up inside my breasts that was removed.

My children and husband picked up the household chores, laundry, cooking, pretty much everything. In my mind, I thought I was going to have a little vacation…. So not true.

On the way to the surgery center, I was blessed with a rainbow. The last thing I remember before being put to sleep, was asking my Guides and Angels to look over me. I visualized healing energy being poured into me.

When I woke up I was dreaming of getting ready to go hiking… I didn't have too much pain… All was great. At home the first two days were easy, rest and a little pain medicine.

I did have drains placed because of the scar tissue removal. These became very cumbersome, very ugly, and I wanted them out. My arm movement was limited. I was also surprised at how tired I was. I had work to do and was functioning at about 20%. The healing process was not so easy after all. The drains stayed in for 10 long days. So, no shower for 10 days.

Slowly, each day I gained a bit more energy. It was a frustratingly longer healing process than I had imagined.

A friend came over while I still had the drains in place. Her comment was very fitting. *Healing is often ugly.* This is so true. Healing from anything can be raw, hard, ugly and vulnerable. Getting rid of the pain, or what caused the pain, can be scary and can be a process that takes commitment and courage.

Last night while comforting one of my children, I was reminded of how difficult healing can be. She is afraid to let go and release her pain. I totally understand and will be there for her. We all have healing to do. Some of it is physical and some of it is emotional. It's all scary. But the recovery feels so good!

I am over joyed with the results of my surgery! I feel like me again and can't wait to work out again.

So, between now and my next letter, another phase of healing will begin in my home.

In closing I wish everyone the courage to heal the pain and find comfort in the reward of recovery.

I know the healing that takes place is not just for us on an individual basis, but a collective whole.

Channeled message

We walk by your side. We lead you and show you the way. We open and close doors for you. We assist you in all the ways you desire. You called upon us at a different place in a different world and we are still connected. One of the greatest misconceptions is life is too short. Life and love extend forever and beyond. What you are giving your attention to is only part of your awareness. You have many experiences, and all are gifts.

We ask that you remember that light is always within and around you. Your truest self, your truest form is always with you and always understands the truth. The truth that you're only light surrounded by energy. This energy is what is serving as your attention. This is what is creating the life you're aware of. Your purpose is to discover how many ways you can share your love and expand. How many ways can you discover the brightness that exists in your soul? What can you create with this energy? You have the unique ability to travel through all of time to be everywhere at once. Because it's all happening now. Allow yourself to experience the love and fortune offered to you time and time again. It has always been with you and always will be. Your own light and love is what guides you through the dark. We rejoice as you discover your true identity. Bask in the light and discover your joy. We are merging together. Our thoughts are becoming stronger and our awareness advancing. It's all now.

End of channel

When I received these words I visually saw a net around my soul. This is our awareness. This can also be recognized as our personal reality. Think "law of attraction" wrapped around your soul. It's more of a filter – it allows things to flow through. But thoughts/denser energy also can get things stuck. This is when healing is needed.

Let's fill our nets with miracles!

savs - Unsplash

Finding the Miracle in Death

MY FAMILY IS recovering from the recent loss of a loved one. We experienced many beautiful moments during the passing of my husband's father. Of course, there are also aspects that leave us feeling sad and at a loss.

One of the beautiful pieces of this story is the time that father, daughter and son were able to share together. My husband and his sister were caring for their dad during his last few days. They were at his side when he passed. Nat King Cole sang *Unforgettable* in the background. Prayers were released for Harold to follow the light. Everyone came together to make this passing both unforgettable and very loving.

At home I lit a candle. Our children shared what they would like their grandfather to experience during his time of transition. The youngest wished his grandfather would eat and drink again… He was not ready to let him go. Our relatives in Norway lit candles in honor of Harold. We were all given time to express our love.

As much as there is a miracle in the beginning of life, there is also a miracle at the end of life. If you believe that we continue on after this life, you know that a new beginning is at hand, with each transition. What we take with us is our absolute love and awareness, what we leave behind is confusion and fear. As we neared his final hours, I could feel the joy and excitement of those on the other side. Harold was being welcomed by many, on his way home.

Channeled message

When the shift of energy occurs, that allows one to cross over, we're all by their side. It is as though they never left. It's impossible to separate love from love. That's how we all stay together. So even when you feel alone or scared, we are always by your side loving you, just as much as the day you were born. Trust that no soul is left behind or not recognized with love. The lessons or growth that occur in this life form are translated into a new comprehension or awareness of love. Each experience is valuable in creating a wholeness of love on the other side. So even loss and sorrow help complete the matrix of the energy that we all are part of. This is what miracles are made of. Whatever you do in this life form, it's translated to love on the other side. Your perceived imperfections or mistakes are eventually translated into lessons that build the matrix of love or source.

Our loved ones take the energy he or she is connected to at the time of crossing. Know that your love and kindness is carried with those that pass. They are aware of your love and only see you in love. They are aware of your sadness; eventually they will only be able to connect to the highest form of you, love. When you're able to share the connection of love with others, including those on the other side, you share an eternal shift to awareness.

End channeling

What I learned during this channel is how each of our experiences is reflected back to us with love. There is nothing that won't be translated or reflected back to our higher selves in love. My logical self is not able to fully comprehend these words. But the images I was shown and the love that I feel during this channel reassures me of our continuation. It also reassures me that truly we're always viewed with love. We are never separated from our loved one. It's only the forms that change. So, when you're missing someone, reach out to them in love. The connection has already been made.

On a side note, I was also shown that when someone crosses over, it's really fast. I was offered the sound and the way it felt to cross over. It is after crossing over that the adjustment comes, but that is when we are surrounded by love.

Soul navigation

How often do we allow ourselves to be guided by the light of our soul? This is even deeper then following one's heart. Our heart carries the love and connection to all, but it is anchored in this life. Our soul offers the wisdom from worlds far away, beyond time and space. Connecting to the awareness of our soul allows us to slip into a world so powerful it pierces through anything not weighted in truth.

All humans carry illusions of time and space. This is one of the hardest transitions to make while living on Earth… Not so as animal, plant or mineral, but as humans. This in part is why many of us have created a life that is not aligned with our true self, our soul. It's as though our internal compass is set differently than the world we exist in. Thankfully every moment is an opportunity to overcome these illusions.

We are offered the presence of timelessness in every instant. Each breath of life is an opportunity to connect. The Earth also offers us opportunities to slow down and reconnect with our soul. Even gravity slows us down and pulls us closer to our truth; closer to the answers many of us seek. As we open up to the possibilities of each moment, our world expands. We're offered the awareness of just being. The gift of recognizing, I AM, the sounds I hear. I AM, the sun I feel. I AM part of both the peace and the doubt.

How do we untangle the peace from the uncertainty? Is it possible to find the root, the very beginning of joy? Can we start from the beginning and painstakingly unwind the fear from joy? Can we release the fear and bring peace closer into all areas of our life? The answer is Yes.

We're often shown in our dreams and in times of contemplation what actions we need to take for our minds to run clear and uninhibited. It might be as simple as decreasing or stopping the consumption of alcohol. It might be as easy as forgiving yourself for deeds done. Certainly it will involve turning your concerns over to your personal team of Angels and guides. It also involves slowing down and connecting to the rhythm of the Universe through meditation.

We watch how you struggle to come to grips with your accomplishments and your dreams. We're here to answer your prayers and to carry your love throughout the world. If we had but one message for you to share it would be, Create! Create with all your heart and soul. Let the flow of love guide you in your creations. Understand that it is through your creativity that God and Angels and your divine energy and life purpose flows. We literally can flow through your fingers to help share messages of good fortune and guidance. We can offer you the ideas that help you create music or find the words of inspiration to share with others. Creativity is what sets the soul free.

Connecting with your soul will bring you to an awareness that cause shifts in all areas of your life and even those you love. It's what brings about the possibility of both peace and tranquility. Imagine trusting yourself to dive into the unknown and taking apart your thoughts and feelings and restructuring them with an awareness of light and purpose. You have the ability to share a life that includes being present for all. This pierces through the shell of protection of your heart that will reconnect you with your soul.

Your soul's energy is new and fresh and will paint your world with colors and feelings never experienced. You will hear, see and feel the scars from your past as they are removed from your emotional energy. You will connect with feelings of inspiration that will guide you. Your very purpose is to live life free of fear. Share your unique individual energy and light.

We're here to help you unravel the words, ideas, and history that has limited your vision. We're here to answer each call for help. It's no longer necessary for you to live with blinders on. Reach out and trust that each of you is blessed with guidance and love and each of you can truly do no wrong. The scars from your past will be removed. You will forever be changed when you dare listen to your soul.

Your soul has been with you forever. It contains the brilliance of all love and the capacity of all light. It also contains the capacity of all grief. The freedom of healing that comes from the expression of love benefits us all.

Take a step further and remove not only the scars in your life but the scars of all humanity. As we practice living in peace with this life, we're lifting the scars of all lifetimes of mankind. As we live a life of personal awareness we begin to bring consciousness into all lifetimes. Each wound that is healed in your life heals a wound in us all. It really is true each person can change the course of humanness.

We want to help you unwind your fears from your life. We want to help you express your dreams the way you see fit. We want to help you create a world that best supports you. The closer you come to achieving your life free of fear and confusion, the closer you come to existing in the awareness of the moment. There is no beginning and no end.

Imagine removing the scars from your past and replacing them with steps taken towards your dreams. Imagine taking these removed scars and fears and setting them free. You have no limitations. Your fears are replaced with an awareness of your successes. You're now able to reframe your life, acknowledging your bravery and how many obstacles you have overcome and how close you are to living a life that allows you to share your inspiration and creativity.

Take your fears and wounds from your past and release them to your Angels and guides. Watch them turn into clarity and wisdom to guide you forward. From this moment on you are brilliance and light soul energy. This is the stuff miracles are created from.

End channeling

London Scout - Unsplash

The Importance of Hope

For as long as I can remember I have put more value on the presence of Faith over the presence of Hope. I live my life in Faith of a greater power. This is what I always fall back on. Until lately, I didn't give much consideration to the capacity of Hope.

My appreciation and awareness of Hope has been building. The first moment of awareness took place a few weeks ago. I watched a stranger reach out to help someone in need. I heard him say, "There is always hope." I felt the energy around us change. The power of his words almost brought me to my knees. Seriously. They carried such kindness and love. I was reminded of the power in the word, Hope.

Hope is something that is shared. This is what makes it invincible. It builds as it is passed between us. It can start as a whisper shared between strangers. It can grow to men and women and children all coming together in solidarity.

Hope Unites Us.

Globally we have experienced floods, fires, and wars. This doesn't even touch the social distress. I finally recognize the importance of hope. We are living in a time that calls for us to share hope, unite together, and overcome fear. Defeating social injustices and panic is not new to us. We've done it in the past. We'll do it again.

What we have in our favor, to completely wipe out fear once and for all, is the awareness of collective thought. Mankind has advanced to the understanding that our thoughts create our reality. It's the power of hope that can unite our thoughts into creating a world of peace and awareness. This is our birthright. We can create together. I believe. I have faith. I have hope.

A few things that have given me hope lately:

I love the fact that Florida Congressional Candidate Bettina Rodriguez Aguilera says she was abducted by aliens. The message she tells is all about love. She has my vote!

We're seeing more people standing up for what they believe in. People are saying no to racism and sexism and other crap. We're starting to listen and be heard.

I'm so thankful for everyone that has helped rescue animals and people in our most recent floods and fires.

I'm thankful for that one person who takes time to offer a stranger hope. It happens all the time.

I think hope comes to life when I share messages from loved ones during my readings. Often these are unexpected, and it makes the moment even sweeter.

Channeled message

We're emerging into an era or understanding of connection that is not literal, a way that is based on feelings alone. Discovering this realm is rich in power and in the feelings of ancient sufferings and confusions and new beginnings. We can only find a way through the patterns of awkwardness and confusion if we allow our heart energy, and our soul energy to lead us.

Imagine you're opening your heart and connecting to all the love and light around you. Your soul is able to speak volumes and not only rescue you from this place of arrogance and injustice but pull you into a place of beauty where you are panic free, free of holding back.

We ask you to hold out your arms. Hold out your hands to the possibility that you alone are the answers that all have been waiting for. You alone hold the secrets to mankind. You alone have the ability to unwind and unleash the power that resides within us all.

When we say "you alone" it is to remind you that we are all a part of you. We are so interconnected and joined together. There's no way to separate you and I.

We're bringing this up again because you have the ability to function on a new plane, a new realm of existence and appreciation. Some call it love. (We have a different form of communication that uses sounds differently.) You will return to the understanding of higher sounds. More colors. This allows you to travel. You will become lighter and find that as you shift through the sound barrier and layers of dense energy, you are removed. You feel free. You're less encumbered. You're carrying less toxins and empty life burdens.

We call to your awareness the possibility of living in the emergence of light.

End of channel

There is more than one message in this channeling. The first is the reminder of our existence other than our human form and our deep connection.

The second message is how colors and sounds and feelings all merge together as one. Imagine putting a piece of tangerine in your mouth. You will experience the color, smell and taste as one vibration. It simplifies our ability to share and experience feelings. This might be related to the absence of fear. We will have no feelings, words, or thoughts of fear.

Past Travels

I'M SO EXCITED for my trip to Southern California. I'm ready to escape the crazy weather in Anchorage, Alaska. It's similar to the crazy energy swirling around our political world. I just want to remind everyone it will be OK. I could go into all the things that appear to be failing, but I won't. I know it will all be OK. This is one of those times when faith can step in and lead you to a more comfortable place. We need to remember that there is so much more going on in our Universe than we can comprehend. So, under these circumstances, Faith and Grace are here to guide us.

On a side note:

Try imagining turning off some aspects of your senses when you want to connect with higher vibrations. We automatically turn things off in our mind when meditating. Our logical mind decreases, and this allows us to connect with other energy. So instead of trying to open up, try shutting down. Shut down the part of you that is often on overload, by loud sounds, other people, electronic devices etc. Try shutting things down by spending more time in nature, or listening to mellow music.

Spend time alone. Create a little personal sanctuary. Basically, decrease the things that agitate you… Even for an hour a day. See if you start experiencing anything fun and unusual. Let me know how this goes.

Austin Schmid - Unsplash

Part II: Processes

What's Your Fear Factor?

WE ALL HAVE dreams and goals. Some of us have clearly defined goals. Others have desires of some vague success. Either way, if the goals are not attained, we are stuck somewhere wanting them. Let's be clear, some people will remain in the early process of achieving and never experience the satisfaction of success. If we're actively working towards our goals, we will have celebrations along the way. We will experience feelings of triumph on our personal path.

We all have fears. These fears can be tied to many experiences in our life. Some fears we can identify, and some remain nameless. We all create both thoughts of fear and of success. The trick is to create thoughts and actions of success, much more then thoughts of fear. Recognizing your ability to achieve greatness must be greater than your fears.

Ask yourself the following questions:

- Are your goals clearly defined?

- Are you actively working on your goals?
- What are the top three goals that you want to achieve?

When working towards achieving your goals:

- Do you have any identifiable fears?
- Is there one big fear that is preventing you to live to your highest potential?

Which is greater:

Your fear factor,

Or

Your success factor?

What are the end results of your goals?

Do you know what you want to do with your life?

How do you want to live, and what is the guiding force in your life?

When you really want to get the answer, who do you turn to?

There are lots of different places where we seek answers – family, friends, life coaches, etc. These options can be very helpful. I hope you also take some time to turn inward. You can ask your questions before you fall asleep or prior to meditation. You can ask your angels and guides... out loud or silently in your mind anytime you want!

Here is a message from our Angelic helpers.

> Throughout the ages, many times people have tried, to no avail, to put an end to humanity or the human evolution. Trust that again we will not allow confusion to hinder your purpose of displaying love and beautiful passages, art and scholarly progress. We are fascinated by the perseverance of mankind to share their gifts. Time and time again a storm arises and it will be followed by the rainbow of light that carries the energy of love... of connection and wholeness..
>
> I want to tell you the story of a little boy born long ago. This story is of Jesus and the many Christ-like saviors that have come to this world time and time again to bless the world with such compassion and wisdom and completeness. The time is upon us again. There are many individuals who are here in this time to lead the way to peace...
>
> Years ago, there was a boy name Jesus. He lived a very simple life. His dad was a cobbler; his mother washed clothes. They shared their bread with the poor. The father was a gifted story teller. The boy grew up hearing these stories of faraway places. The boy had a desire to travel and share stories, but also to care for his aging parents.
>
> The boy was shown in a vision his parents would be cared

for. He began his journey of traveling and telling stories, never sure where he would stay at night or where his food would come from. He followed the guidance of his angels, never losing faith in his journey. Never believing it was more than an adventure that entailed sharing stories and prophecies to the villages he traveled to...

His following became much greater. He never lost sight of his basic desire to spread the word of compassion and the energy of love. He knew his needs were being met. He knew his parents were being cared for. He had faith and trusted in the will of God, per the conversation with his Angels. As his following grew on Earth his following of Angels grew in Heaven. He began noticing his abilities to transcend his body. His energy was changing as his group of Angels grew. He was able to perform miracles.

This is not to say strife did not exist for him – quite the contrary. But he never allowed the strife to affect his goal of sharing love and compassion. In fact, he believed it was part of the process. He learned that some beings people need to experience strife to make sense of what they have in their life. Some beings need to experience what they consider a loss. It helps heal a place deep inside. Loss can be a tool for learning that you're enough as you are. Seek for answers no farther then deep inside you. This is where you connect with the divine. You always have your team of Angels and guides at your side. The more you connect with the Angelic community, the more angels and guides you have just waiting to assist you.

Truthfully, there is no end to this story. It's replayed every day. You all have the ability to connect and spread the words of compassion, strength and courage. Know that if you're sharing your gifts of love, gratitude and insight, you're just where you should be… helping the Angels. And you in turn will always be guided and protected.

We ask that you take time daily to connect to your personal guidance. Trust in the process. You're brought into this world with the collective energy of love. This energy can grow and guide you throughout life. Imagine being placed in the center of this divine energy… It's always with you. You can increase it by actively working with your angels and guides. You will notice more and more miracles at hand.

Many Angels and guides are waiting for you to summon them…

Much love from your collective Angel community.

In closing, take the time to trust yourself. Start calling on your Angels. You have everything you need inside.

End message

On a side note, I know that there are many teachers from many religions and even many teachers that are not affiliated with a religion at all. Yet this little story came through when I asked for guidance and so I wanted to share it.

Dial in the frequency of Love

I HAVE BEEN BACK in Alaska almost a week. I noticed it took me a few days to calibrate to the energy difference between California and Alaska. Both places have things that I enjoy. I just found this time to take me a couple days to settle in and feel good.

This feeling of not being celebrated is similar to how many people feel in their every-day life. They are not completely settled in. Do you ever feel uncomfortable with your surroundings? Or even out of touch with what's going on? I have a few ideas about why this happens. One is we're connected to the past in this life or even very connected to energy of the other side.

How do we get more settled in this life? Prayer and meditation are the easiest ways. Find a small area in your home, that you can turn into your sanctuary. This will be your place to start to feel good again. At least once daily settle in, breath, close your eyes and hand off your burdens to a higher source. Just let them go. Recognize how it feels to release your problems. Imagine that in your space, you're able to relinquish anything that no longer serves you. In return you are filled with love, healing and wellness. You're fully supported and thriving in all areas of your life. Your very being is being touched by loving energy.

As you grow more comfortable with this feeling of connection to higher energy, increase the size of your sanctuary. This is done by removing clutter in your home. Also, practice meditation and prayer in other parts of your home. The goal over time is that you will develop a wonderful sense of self as well as a deeper connection to our divine energy. You will be able to take this self-love with you wherever you go. Imagine always being nurtured and protected while you explore and grow. Mostly I encourage the act of self-care and self-love. You deserve it!

Channeled message

There is much cause for celebration. We have an amazing amount of love and light in many forms encircling you and encircling Earth. This is energetically a very exciting time. We are helping you manifest and connect. It's easier now than ever before to connect to the higher vibrational shifts. It's easier to help recover your sense of self. Small adjustments can cause a great appearance of love and light in your life. You will notice different sounds or even feel the vibrations. Trust us; it will make complete sense.

This frequency change to love causes some chaos. But between the chaotic events bears the opening to a greater version of your world. Believe us, there is energy stored in many places that will begin to shift., in the climate, the rocks and dirt, below the water. In your lifetime, you will see many great changes which occur that allow for the vibration of peace and love to heal and nurture. This is a time of great growth. It's also the time of a very young and inexperienced world finding its way to peace.

This is the time of learning we are all connected, everything. And war is too great of a price to pay. The communities at large will realize this. There will be struggles but the great war will be divided by two seas. The outcome will be peace. You will see war, but it will be from across the ocean. The monetary climate is changing. You will see currencies come and go. Trade wars, yes. This is tied to the currency struggles with power or rather loss of power.

I have been given bits and pieces of the above channeled message many times. I do feel like we're in a time of much chaos, but we are given the opportunity to connect with peace during this time. Globally, we will see significant changes. This message of war I have not been given before. The way I see the conflict is there is an ocean between the U. S. and both countries fighting and there is an ocean between them. We will be involved but not on U. S. soil. Another thing I was shown was an active volcano under sea... Is this possible? Again, there is peace that comes out of this chaos. Ultimately, we will all experience peace.

Shahastra - Meeting the Self Reflection Cards

A Clear Mind

Human bodies and minds are amazing as individual systems, but even more so when they unite together. They communicate so seamlessly, it's almost impossible to understand. They operate in perfection at all times. Every thought counts. Each cell, blood vessel, organ and bone knows exactly what to do. The brain, heart and mind work together to keep the human form alive and aware. Our body is a place of many miracles occurring simultaneously.

Our body and mind are both able to adjust, shift and recover. Think about a person who suffers a broken bone. Their body compensates and functions at the highest level possible. Our bodies know how to compensate due to disease and unhealthy lifestyles.

Sometimes our physical selves over-compensate. An anaphylactic reaction is an example of a physical body over-compensating for a perceived threat. The compensation is more dangerous than the original threat.

Our mind (or consciousness) is also able to compensate and

heal. Our conscious mind is the realm of perception. It quickly and efficiently labels situations as good or something to be feared. This helps keep our physical body safe, as well as our emotional body safe. All the experiences of the conscious mind are shared with our subconscious mind. Our subconscious mind has the ability to hold on to everything. It can save all the feelings and emotions of past experiences. Eventually our deepest beliefs will affect our conscious mind.

Our reactions will eventually be based on our subconscious thoughts, feelings and beliefs.

Depending on the health of our subconscious mind, we experience a world of love or fear. Ideally our subconscious will be a place of neutrality. With the practice of meditation and possibly therapy, we can clear our mind of blocks that have settled in. Our subconscious is also our link to experiencing the Law of Attraction and manifesting.

I like to think of our subconscious mind as a resting point for thoughts. It is in this place that we determine if we want the current thoughts or beliefs manifesting in our life.

We should be able to slow down in life enough to connect with our subconscious mind. Our subconscious in its pure state is a place of neutrality. I visualize the subconscious mind holding our highest potential in this life. It's the energy that connects our souls, mind, and heart. It is always ready to manifest a brilliant existence.

Our subconscious minds also carry the imprints from past lives. They are the lessons or karma that brought us back to this physical body. Maybe this lifetime we can clear them for good!

What happens when we experience blocks in our mind?

When we don't have a flow of positive thoughts and vibrations in our mind, our physical self will be affected. For example, if we tell ourselves we are unlovable, our heart may receive messages of fear and lack. Imagine the heart shutting down in an attempt to save the love it currently holds. This is similar to the anaphylactic shock mentioned before. The heart begins to shut down in an attempt to save any loving energy circulating through the body. This shut-down of heart energy triggered by subconscious fears threatens the wellness of the physical self and emotional self.

Blocks or lack of flowing energy in our mind affect our heart and potentially any area in our physical body. Not only do we need to care for our body with sunlight, good nutrition and self-care, but also care lovingly for our mind.

To thrive in our human form, we need to focus on love and the highest vibrational experiences. Practice self-care. Visualize releasing what is blocking your wellness. Connect to only loving, healing energy flowing through your conscious mind, subconscious mind and connect to your superconscious mind.

One of the easiest ways to do this is prayer and meditation.

Energy is contagious. The healthier you are and the more you experience the flow of life energy, the more you will be experience the Super Conscious mind. This is where we connect to the highest vibrations, higher self, and all that is. The Super Conscious is beyond time and space. The super conscious is energy that is found in your heart, mind, soul and all that is;

really everything. The Super Conscious connects you to the light of the Divine.

The Universal Truth Is the Absence of Doubt

WE THINK IT is important for you to understand the majestic part of you that each individual carries. You can imagine this as a light that is in each of your DNA strands. Each of you individually is vital to the whole or the completion of the sound and color formation of the universe. At any given time, you are unconsciously contributing to the spectrum of the energy in our universe. This collective song is what continues to carry messages that tie the past, present and future or the universal whole together. The term past, present and future is for the sake of comprehension …It's all happening now.

Imagine visually the collective song looks like the Northern lights. It's a beautiful field of colorful energy that is always moving and never static. This is much like the collective energy that is emitted from each of you. Each of us carries an important tone in the song of the universe and carries an important color in the spectrum of life.

The Beauty of this individual light is how it holds your essence combined with the light of the universe or God /source. This is your truest self. This is your soul. We want you to treasure and nurture / value your individual awareness / connection to source. This light is collectively your personal journey through all your lives and experiences in all realms. It's your wisdom and greatest accomplishment.

Imagine this light, your soul, always connecting and communicating with source, Angels, and even your loved ones on the other side. Imagine this light is always in the process of activating light in others and exchanging energy with what people think of as Heaven. You are always in contact with your loved ones that have crossed over, your soul group and source.

What does it take for an individual to believe and to garner faith in the heavenly bodies within? We say heavenly bodies within because the light you carry with in is the light of all. Hark back to when you were a little girl or boy and you knew that life from other planes existed. Yes, you knew. You knew you were never alone. You understood the mysteries of the world. There is a time in all lives where an open heart exists. It is an open heart that allows the presence of God in all beings to flourish. As confusion in this life expands we put more awareness on the confusion and less awareness on the bright light that knows universal truth. The universal truth is the complete absence of doubt and confusion.

We are in a time where connecting to doubt is easy. This is truly creating some universal noise. But beyond the noise we all continue to connect to the colors and sounds of love in our collective consciousness.

Why do we want you to know this? We stress that each of you is important to the wholeness of our consciousness. Each of you carries a beauty that is stunning in its glory and completes the universal consciousness. So, when challenges arise, or you find yourself questioning your importance. please remember each of you is treasured and necessary for the completion of our story.

Also imagine that with your first breath this collective light energy settles in near your heart chakra. With your last breath it will leave your physical body. All the breaths between your first and last help keep you connected to your unique place in the Universe.

We think it is important for you to understand the majestic part of you that each individual carries. You can imagine this as a light that is in each of your DNA strands. Each of you individually is vital to the whole or the completion of the sound and color formation of the universe. At any given time, you are unconsciously contributing to the spectrum of the energy in our universe. This collective song is what continues to carry messages that tie the past, present and future or the universal whole together. The term past, present and future is for the sake of comprehension. It's all happening now.

Imagine visually that the collective song looks like the Northern lights. It's a beautiful field of colorful energy that is always moving and never static. This is much like the collective energy that is emitted from each of you. Each of us carries an important tone in the song of the universe and carries an important color in the spectrum of life.

The Beauty of this individual light is how it holds your essence combined with the light of the universe or God /source. This is your truest self. This is your soul. We want you to treasure and nurture / value your individual awareness / connection to source. This light is collectively your personal journey through all your lives and experiences in all realms. It's your wisdom and greatest accomplishment.

Imagine this light, your soul, always connecting and communicating with source, Angels and even your loved ones on the other side. Imagine this light is always in the process of activating light in others and exchanging energy with what people think of as Heaven. You are always in contact with your loved ones who have crossed over, your soul group and source.

What does it take for an individual to believe and to garner faith in the heavenly bodies within? We say heavenly bodies within because the light you carry with inside is the light of all. Hark back to when you were a little girl or boy and you knew that life from other planes existed. Yes, you knew. You knew you were never alone. You understood the mysteries of the world. There is a time in all lives where an open heart exists. It is an open heart that allows the presence of God in all beings to flourish. As confusion in this life expands, we put more awareness on the confusion and less awareness on the bright light that knows universal truth. The universal truth is the complete absence of doubt and confusion.

We are in a time where connecting to doubt is easy. This is truly creating some universal noise. But beyond the noise we all continue to connect to the colors and sounds of love in our collective consciousness.

Why do we want you to know this? We stress that each of you is important to the wholeness of our consciousness. Each of you carries a beauty that is stunning in its glory and completes the universal consciousness. So, when challenges arise, or you find yourself questioning your importance. please remember each of you is treasured and necessary for the completion of our story.

Also imagine that with your first breath this collective light energy settles in near your heart chakra. With your last breath it will leave your physical body. All the breaths between your first and last help keep you connected to your unique place in the Universe.

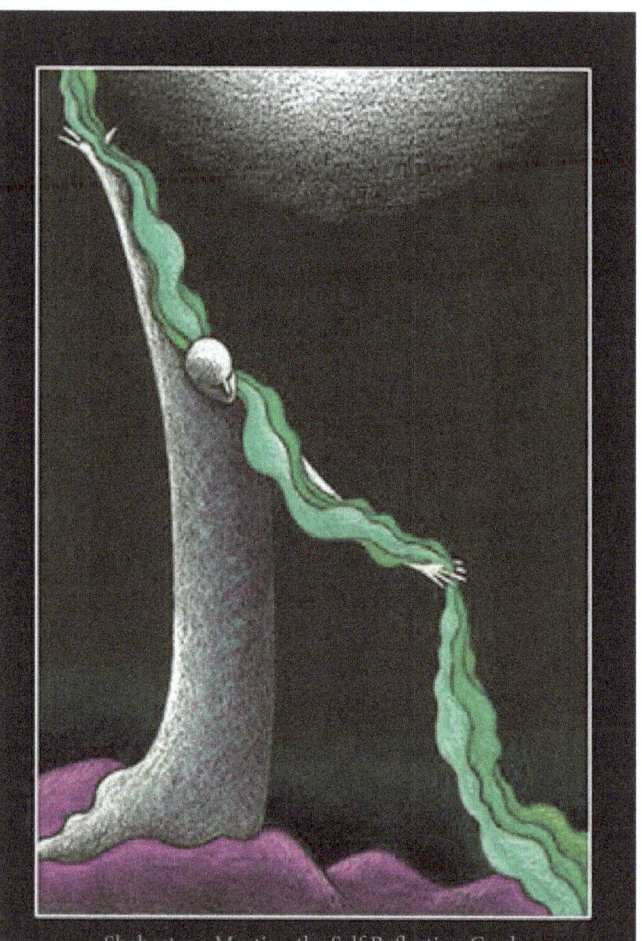

Shahastra - Meeting the Self Reflection Cards

The Sound of Vibrational Change

If you're reading this you must have found a little sacred, safe time and place. Yay you! With our current political climate and overall global activity, it's easy to feel pulled out of balance. Our families, communities and even our world are trying to find their own safe spot. We retreat inward which can be very healing. Take this time to recognize and even honor that which you're taking a break from.

When we retreat inward, we're allowed to make a deeper connection with ourselves. We might not have done that, if we didn't feel the need to heal our energy. So, recognizing what didn't feel good can be healthy. Letting go of what doesn't feel good is healthy. We need to do this for ourselves, our families and our World. Obviously, the more people involved, the greater the challenge. What if we recognized all the pieces of our self, community and world and decided how they work together. Release the pieces that are too sharp and bless them on their journey.

It's possible to look at something that causes pain, like disease, in a whole new way. Imagine taking the disease out of your body. You can have gratitude for how it potentially brought your family closer. You can have gratitude for how it helped you realize the beauty in your life. You can then release the fragments of the disease that don't serve you. Send them off to the Universe to be taken care of.

I'm using this same tool when I look at our political climate. I recognize what is going on. I take note of what doesn't feel good. I'm also thankful for how some of the ugly situations are being recognized for what they are. We need to make room for healing energy to come in and have faith that what is not in our highest good will be released.

We have the power to put the pieces together in our life however we want. So, pull into your safe spot and do inventory of what you're keeping and what you're releasing. Take the time to really connect to all the pieces and people in your life and see if they still fit. Celebrate the success of things coming together!!

Channeled message

If this resonates with you, we want you to understand the collective process of letting go and stepping back. As you let go of fears, even wants and desires, allow yourself to feel how they are released. Allow the universe to take care of you. It's a dance of letting go and having faith your dreams will be realized. You've already been gifted with the absolute best version of your dreams. Let go of the fear and hold space for the blessings. We're equipped to help you release your fears, so you only experience the essence of love. First you must be willing to do so. Your will is your gateway to the

highest vibrational energy. Claiming what has been offered is so powerful… You're given multiple chances and endless opportunities to discover expanded versions of yourself.

The blessings will continue and are on the rise as you connect with the higher vibrational energy. Your awareness shifts to recognizing only the blessings. Nothing else is a match in this high vibrational state. We are always pulling and twisting the energy to help carry the beautiful thoughts and prayers to the highest point possible for mankind to touch. Your essence is already experiencing vibrational buoyancy….

The following piece is a message for someone preparing for transition:

You're beginning to experience vibration buoyancy. You have the ability to float and adjust to the sounds and images of love and light. Let us help you find your way. Sounds of healing and miraculous energy pulls your complete essence into a higher vibrational state. We will help you receive love and light with a completely open heart. You have the ability to flow and adjust to the sounds we share, to the colors we share, to the images and love that we share. As you adjust to the sacred energy of source, we're with you, holding your hand, helping you experience and re-experience the transition of life and after life. You're never alone. We help adjust to your new abilities and adjust to the new expansion you're able to experience. You will remember yourself; there never was a separation. We were with you all along.

(The way I'm shown our essence after passing is almost a vision of simply thoughts. It's an absence of anything but thoughts. However, the thoughts are so loving and healing and can't be described by my words. You can feel the thoughts of others, similar to the way I currently work with energy.)

So, for now, rest, recover, heal and know that you're loved and appreciated. This is your journey, but not yours alone. You lit the fire for many and adjusted the light for others. The story continues; your light continues to shine as bright as ever. You will be carried forever in the hearts of loved ones and in the minds of others. You put the pieces together beautifully. Blessings…

End of Channel

Sensitivity is beautiful!

Not long ago I was contacted by someone who felt like they were one of the few sensitive people in our world. They struggled with others treating them differently. At times they got lost in the pain of the world. Believe me, I can relate! But I choose to celebrate our ability to feel. Sensitivity is beautiful.

I believe sensitivity makes us aware and connected. It allows compassion to guide us in this life. One of the wonderful pieces of sensitivity is how it connects us to the moment. Imagine being so aware that you actually stop and connect to what is around you. You just might find things at this moment are perfect…

Sensitivity can also guide you to peace. Experiencing life with heightened sensitivity is one of the joys of living. Being receptive to the energy around you invigorates your energy field, making it vibrant and healthy!

Sensitivity is also a tool. Let it direct you away from what doesn't feel good. This is why we have the ability to feel. It's a gift to help you create your ideal life. The more you use it, the better your world becomes.

One of the challenges that comes with being sensitive is to keep fear from rerouting or diminishing your ability to feel. If you have a bad experience, just acknowledge it and keep the lesson. Don't hold on to the bad feelings and let fear dictate your choices. To live in this world as a sensitive person takes courage! You feel not just your own experiences but those of others as well. You are so much more aware of our possibilities. You have the ability to make decisions not just how it feels to you, but how it will affect others.

Don't change yourself to fit into a small world. Expand and allow your true expression to create a vibrant healthy world. Humanity needs compassion and awareness. Imagine if our world leaders allowed sensitivity to guide them instead of fear. We would be free of wars, boarders and fear. We're blessed at this time with many sensitive people joining us on Earth. They are courageous and living life to the fullest. Let us all celebrate sensitivity however it appears in our life.

Channeled message

Ask your Angels and guides to help you maintain a balance when increasing your sensitivity. We can help you adjust to the higher vibrations of the energy around you. The word balance comes to mind when speaking of sensitivity. To live a life of awareness allows balance to flow into your life. You become aware of your connection to all. We can guide you into a life free of judgment and

pain. Many people struggle with letting go of fear and the

idea of lack. This is why sensitivity was created. When you step out of limited awareness you are guided to help create a shift in the universal consciousness.

Think small in terms of this change. It requires nothing more of you than to live in the moment. Breathe and check in with how you feel. Do you feel connected to those around you? Ask to connect to the higher vibrational energy.

Be courageous and share this expanded version of you. You will soon experience new possibilities, new friends and an entirely new world. You will begin to attract what feels good to you. Remember to separate sensitivity from the fear. They are completely different things. One will expand your world view. One will diminish your perceived potential. It's all about letting go of the fear and celebrating the ability to always be guided into new frequencies.

Shahastra - Meeting the Self Reflection Cards

Call to Mind

Meditation

May each of us feel more in tune with our soul's energy and our ability to express our individual brilliance.

You are fully supported in this life, in this room, in this moment.

Take a deep breath and fully exhale. Release any tension you might be holding.

Take another deep breath and exhale, releasing anything else that might be feeling heavy.

Recognize that each breath in is filled with pure radiant light. Each breath is filled with the lightest and highest frequency possible.

Just as every breath released, is allowing you to relinquish anything that is not for your highest good.

You are fully supported by our loving Earth Energy. Feel this grounding energy coming in and filling you up. This Earth Energy is your anchor to staying balanced during your time on Earth. It brings you steady focus and resiliency and strength for your physical self. This strong beautiful energy blends with your heart and soul to help you achieve your dreams. Allow yourself to sink deeper into the welcoming energy of our beautiful Earth.

As you sink deeper into the Energy of the Earth your body is relaxing and settling into a state of allowing. Each breath is drawing to you a radiant cosmic energy. This cosmic energy flows into every part of you. Your heart is opening up. You are becoming aware of the messages your heart and soul carry for you to share.

As your heart is opening and receiving the healing energy of love, you're releasing anything not of love.

As your heart continues to untangle any trapped dense energy you're being bathing in the light of the Divine. You are filled with sacred energy that calms fears. You recognize your true brilliance.

Each breath brings you closer to realizing your true divine nature.

Experience the calming effect of healing. Feel yourself slip deeper into a place that is filled with love and light. You might even be able to look down at your human form and acknowledge the gift of this human life.

Knowing that everything is just as it should be. This moment is perfect. You are healed. You are loved. You are free to express your divine self.

The beautiful Earth Energy is holding space for your heart and soul to create the perfect space for your healing to continue. The cosmic energy surrounds you and creates the perfect channels for Divine messages to be shared with you. This moment is perfection.

Know that you are loved.

Settle in and call to your mind any messages that are yours to keep close to your heart. Call to mind any messages that are meant to be shared.

Shahastra - Meeting the Self Reflection Cards

Empowered

MY DECLARED SEASON of healing has brought many wonderful things into my life. I've also experienced some interesting surprises. I am joyfully celebrating my successes and learning to let go of my frustrations. I'm firmly on my healing path.

Currently, I am with my youngest in the Seattle area. We arrived on Sunday for an overnight swim camp. He was a little worried about attending on his own. We talked about it as he fell asleep next to me. In the morning his attitude had changed. My 11-year-old was ready for his adventure to begin.

The way my son is able to let go of his fears is enviable. He felt safe expressing his fears and then was able to release them. How would each of our lives look if we could safely express our fears and let them go? What if we all had the courage to try new things? I'm talking about the things you dream of.

Hopefully you have a network of friends or family you can turn to for encouragement and love.

Thankfully we all have a spiritual team and Universal Energy to help us create our magnificent lives.

The key word is create. Trust yourself in knowing what is good for your soul experience. If you truly trust yourself and your connection, you will create an amazing adventure. If you don't trust yourself and your connection, you will still create. It just might not feel as good. Everything you have right now, you have created. Do you feel empowered or alarmed?

I view source as an omnipresent love in all our lives and beings. We can always turn inward to connect to this energy. Wherever you are, the connection remains. This connection brings healing and strength into our world on a personal and global level. It also brings the awareness that we all have the ability to create and attract what fills our days. Remembering this connection can offer you the courage to live life joyfully. When the fear is gone, you know you can create a rewarding experience. Even if the first time you don't get it right, the opportunities are still waiting for you. Keep trying! Learning how to create and work with energy is a lifelong experience.

It's important to practice the concept of connecting to source and living with faith. Live your life knowing that you're here to succeed. You're here to experience joy, love, courage and passion. You're so powerful that you can attract into your life exactly what you put your time and energy into. Pay attention to your thoughts. Live courageously and commit to creating an expanded version of your world. Remember – practice makes perfect.

Let the light shine through the veil of confusion. This confusion is fear. It's the only thing that separates you from absolute awareness of your light energy. Imagine removing clouded thoughts and disbelief and revealing light where darkness once was.

Slowly we wrap light and healing love around you as you sleep. We listen to your words and feel your dreams. We feel your joy, not your fear. We hold you so dearly to our heart, always. You're filled with the beautiful energy of source. We experience each breath you take and release. Your journey has just started.

We allow you to expand and grow at your chosen pace. It's your journey. We watch over you, but never step in the way of your actions, until we're asked to do so. All you need to do is ask. We have no connection to fear, only love. We see and experience only light. Every step of your journey we connect with your light energy. The essence of you is light. This allows you to easily shift from fear. There is no connection to fear in your purest form. You travel through many worlds as pure light form. In your truest form, you've never expressed fear or needed to express fear. You're experiencing a creation of many lives over and over and over. It's as simple as breathing one breath; you can release fear and master your lives, all your lives. There is no karma too strong, no loss too great, to overcome your beautiful light. Create with joy in mind and see what unfolds. Experience this life with the awareness that all life forms are connected. All life forms share the brilliance of discovering their light.

End Channeled Message

In this message I became aware that fear is something we as humans have created. As we become more aware of our potential and attract higher vibrational energy, there is no fear. The better we understand our true nature, the more we create an absence of fear. You won't be able to attract what you can't imagine and feel. So, in closing, choose empowered thoughts. Go where you experience courage, love and light.

New Beginnings

ONE THING I have learned for sure. Life is never boring when you have a family. This can be your family of origin or the family you're guiding into adulthood. It doesn't matter how these people come into your life, they come chock-full of life lessons. In the past month or so, I have laughed so hard I cried with my family. I have also had moments that brought me to tears. This is real. This is my life.

I declared a season of healing for the next few months. I now realize it's a lifetime of healing. I had my little checklist of what I wanted to tackle this summer. As I have mentioned, I wanted true, significant healing, true exploration of feelings and communication. One of my big goals was for our family of five to all spend more time together. We're all busy and have our own individual commitments. I was looking for a pledge from all five members.

I recognize it was my goal. Most of the family was on board. One of my children is similar to how I was in my younger years. Unless it involves the promise of intrigue, a little risk and laughter, she's not interested. Freedom and hippy busses are her goals. I can understand where she is… not far from my place about 30 years ago. I didn't push too much on increasing her time at home. I was getting frustrated, but waited to see how it would all come together.

The past week most of my family headed North for a swim meet and also to spend time near Denali. The young hippy child wanted to stay home for work. She was also planning to have a girlfriend stay with her. I was disappointed. I actually told her to call in sick. (I still have a bit of rebel, or whatever in me). She stood her ground and said she was staying home to earn money. Ha Ha.

As I mentioned previously, on one particular evening, my daughter had a bad experience and learned some valuable life lessons. Our entire family was affected. At first there was blaming. We eventually all came together and worked as a team to recover from a weekend we will never forget. Our daughter is fine. It opened her eyes to some of the craziness you can experience.

The blessing in this – she is now spending a lot of time at home. She is grounded, for a long time. The crazy weekend gifted me and my family of five a bonding experience. It also brought a lot of communication between siblings and parents. I think it even helped my daughter grow up a little. I'm sharing this story to demonstrate that when we ask for something, we never know how it will show up. This event brought my family to the exact place I desired. Did I want the crappy part of the weekend? Absolutely not! But it brought us to a really good starting point for growing closer. And one day we will laugh about it. We have a camera system that shared the variety of people and actions in our home. Most of the craziest night in history is on tape!

Channeled message

The scripture doesn't display the amount of knowledge that collectively we all hold. This is the true moment of discovery. You now all know. There is no need for continuing lessons when a balance of heart, mind and soul guide you through life.

To understand this, think of compassionate existence as just pure light energy, no physicality. You're this… You also have the ability to continue to learn and explore the different ways of expression of self, self of the human body, self of the human spirit, self of the soul. All experiences and expressions lead to the beauty of growth. It's all now. We want you to continue exploring until you experience the point of complete satisfaction of learning love in all ways, shapes and forms. Expanded love is always pure, judgment free, pure light energy. there is not a physical form of pure expanded love… You connect the feelings of love to images, such as a mother with newborn baby. Yet love is found in all images… That is your gift. Explore the idea of finding love in all images. It's there waiting for you. Ask for help, we will guide you to the point of love that can't even be comprehended. love of all that is.

Understanding the light energy all around you, with in you, and of you… This love, light, compassion and joy are indescribable. You're all that and more. We're all, that and more. Shifting your awareness to the expansion of energy will bring you closer to the experiences you desire. It's a process of replacing fear, judgment and loss with connection of recognizing you as all that is. Finding yourself in a moment of clarity and joy is all there truly is. Let everything else go and just experience the connection.

The human body is a tool and sometimes a shield. It can allow or prohibit the comprehensions and expansiveness of love. Many are getting so close to the tipping point of recognizing and staying in the light, of the light, being light. It's all possible now!

End of channeling

Part III: Results

The Vibration of Peace

Did you know that you're evolving at a faster pace than ever before? Evolution is taking place inside you, around you and because of you. You hold the key element of this light energy inside you. Take a moment and close your eyes.

Imagine the essence of you, your core energy, your heartrending, beautiful self, being brought closer and closer to the surface of your physical body. Imagine this self breaking through past beliefs, past hurts. Imagine this true you, finally believing and acknowledging that you have completed this aspect of your journey. You are ready to live a life of awareness, of love and compassion and brilliance.

Imagine this true you finally settling into the warmth and the love of all that exists. Imagine the true you recognizing your love, your strength your perfect self. You're now ready to open up and share your enlightened heart and mind. Know that every step of the way has been worth it. You have been guided to this very moment, by this very breath. This realization has been guiding you to eternity. Honor this very real part of you. Press your hands to your heart. Breathe deep.

We have always been with you. Allow yourself to be healed and to explore this new energy that is you. Your highest you. Reach before you, reach around you, and draw in this love. We, your guides and angels have been seeking you. This realization, this dawning within you, might come and go, but we will remain by your side. You will again remember this realization of self-awareness and self-love. Rest your fears. Open up to a complete healing of the soul. Let us guide you. Peace, compassion, awareness – these are words that can't sufficiently describe what waits for a heart that is opening.

We will always allow the needed shifts to occur for your happiness and well-being. We delight in your ability to explore the energetic realm in so many ways. When you tire, we will be waiting for you. To lift you up and take you home, where you have always been. Your true self awaits.

The above message was created as a tool for those seeking to connect with eternal love and the vibration of peace. We wait for you always.

Winning

I RECENTLY ENTERED TO win a prize at the gym I attend. It was a month-long contest. Each time I attended the gym, I thought about how I was going to win. I pre-planned how I would share my prize. When the final day rolled around I was ready. My family was not surprised when a text confirmed that I had won! Truthfully the prize was not going to change my life, but it did make me feel good.

We can all live life enjoying winning moments and abundance.

Here's the deal. We can all win and experience abundance. It's the attitude we carry with us that dictates a win or not. For example, the fact that I'm able to work out in a gym is what I'm really celebrating. Winner or loser, it's all in my mind. I celebrate winning however it comes into my life. I also celebrate winning when it comes into the lives of others. We all have an eternity of personal and global winning moments.

I asked my youngest what he thinks about winning at swim meets. His response was perfect. He considers making his goal times a win. He also loves to do well in an event. It's really all about the fact that he loves swimming. As parents, we win because we share his joy. When he found something he gets excited about, he won in the game of life. I could follow the trail of how we have been winning for years, but you get the picture.

There were many winning moments during the recent flood in Texas. We were able to witness humanity coming together to help each other. People risked their lives to save those in need; including animals. Observing strangers courageously work together for a common cause, is a beautiful global win!

Sometimes getting a rejection can be a win. It might not seem so at the moment. Those difficult times or let downs often lead us to a place where we will thrive. Imagine not getting a job you really wanted. Maybe this will inspire you to return to college where you experience many winning moments and eventually get that dream job.

In my mind we can prepare for winning our entire life. It's getting excited about every little win that makes way for the big wins. Remember if you believe you deserve to win, you're already preparing for your next win. Here is one more thought…

If you're not enjoying something and feel like you're never winning, does it still belong in your life?

Maybe it's time to find a different perspective or even a different job, partner etc. We should always hold in our heart the strong possibility of winning. This welcomes gratitude and excitement into our life. A good friend just shared these words, "Anticipation is absolutely lovely." And so it is.

Enjoy the remaining sunny days. Prayers for all of us to be gently guided into a world of compassion and peace.

*****

Channeled message

Sifting through the sounds that clutter your mind, you can connect to one thought, one moment that helps you focus and clearly sense your life. Everyday life holds so many magical moments. Take the time to exhale and let your breath join you to this moment. Imagine your breath and your thoughts colored by emotions spread out across forever.

What if your thoughts, much like your breath, are able to travel across distances and churn with the thoughts of others to complete a patchwork of wisdom and kindness that will last for generations? What if all your thoughts of now are willing you to remember other times, even future times of peace and tranquility? What if it's only your thoughts that are capable of creating a discipline of peace and awareness resting all throughout our world and the shift occurs now?

All else falls away.

End of channel

Super charged Energy

THE OTHER DAY I left my house for a quick errand. It was probably about 10 degrees Fahrenheit, with snow on the ground. I slipped my feet into my son's shoes. I had the funniest sensation. His shoes contained so much of his I felt like him. I trotted out the door and vibrated with his goofy, 11-year-old energy. His happy, carefree energy was easy for me to recognize.

This reminded me of how we all carry super-charged energy with us. We all share our energy (and receive each other's energy) and we all contribute to the collective energy. Be aware of what feels good, and if something doesn't feel good, shut it down, or take the shoes off.

Channeled message

In a neutral state, there is no right or wrong. There is only the presence of grace. This state of neutrality can call forth an amazing amount of powerful energy to create a life that allows the highest vibrational energy to flow in and create an existence where beauty and eloquence of soul matter. A world where only the truest concept of love and light are allowed to thrive. A place within you that holds the most powerful, sweetest, truest form of love, of God and all that is.

Surrounding God is a place of neutrality. In this area that is of God and yet not aware of the connection, there is neither good nor bad. Knowing that you can find and connect to God within yourself, you can also find and connect to God in all. Nothing exists without the presence of God.

We each also have the ability to experience emptiness. The place of emptiness and fear do not truly exist. Our minds have created time and space, a place where fear can cultivate. It's when we go to our truest form of self; free of time and space, that we connect to all that is. God. The place of neutrality that connects to God, grows and expands into a greater form of self.

End of Channel

I hope this finds everyone in a blissful state!

Shahastra - Meeting the Self Reflection Cards

Filip Mroz - Unsplash

Our Consciousness is Everything

Upon returning to Alaska, I find myself being drawn to the feelings I experienced on a recent trip to Hawaii. I'm so grateful for all the little pieces that came together and helped me figure out what works for me. The next step is getting the resolve to create a life that is even more supportive of my mind, body and soul.

With that in mind, are you aware of what fully supports your mind, body and soul? Do you have the resolve to create a life that supports you? This can be tough. Lots of people find themselves at a loss in relationships, poor health, and experiencing lack. Where did it all unravel and how do you rebuild? This is a life long journey of balance, trust and self-love.

First things first, care for yourself. Meditate, pray, eat healthy foods, rest. Allow creativity to guide you in life. Do more of what makes you happy. Find a group that supports you and your life style. Choose one of these things and do it daily. Slowly add more of these basic care life ingredients into your life. Trust that you're worth the changes that need to take place for a life of wellness. P.S. This can be as easy as meditating daily.

Channeled message

The energetic shift… Our Universe is made up of frequencies of emotions and feelings (think of matter being made of up thoughts, feelings and emotions), all the changes in the universe (your life) are in response to our (your) energetic feelings. To understand this, it's where we allow our minds to go that produces the shift of insight. Thus, when you spend time in peaceful studies or peaceful actions this bring peace to all your awareness and your life experiences, your awareness is the depth of your spiritual mind.

All beings have available the same energy, be it a guide or angel or person. There is no difference, except the ability to see an expanded, deeper version of what energy is. Spiritual beings are made up of your energy and vice versa. This allows us (Angels, Guides) to communicate with you, to be you. We are you.

We wish you to realize that the absolute genuine love and compassion that exists within us, is in you also and it's always available. Our guidance and support are always available. Again, this is how we communicate with you. You release your thoughts, emotions – we respond. To understand this on a bigger picture, it's not so much separate energy responds, but your more aware energy responds

through the universal energy. For example, when you're sending out thoughts to the universe, it is you that delivers the response from the universe, and remember the universe is you.

To understand this on a greater level, just be aware that there is no separation. We're all energy, everything. So when you communicate with angels and guides, you're communicating with a higher source of you. Our entire energy source is love and adoration. And yet we find the need to explore the what ifs… What if we're not all love? What if we're sick? What if….?

Don't worry so much about the state of mind of others. We all exist in harmony at any given moment. Remember that there is no difference in how things are created, be it a cow, human, planet, stone. We all exist in this perfect understanding and balance because we're all one.

End Channel

This was very interesting to me because I'm sure now there is no separation between myself and the energy that shares messages with me. We often hear there is no separation, but to understand on a level that acknowledges us to be the same energy as source, angels, divine beings is more difficult. I guess it sums it up to say we are all spiritual beings in all ways, always.

Erik Odiin - Unsp

Circle of Divinity

I HAVE BEEN INSPIRED to dedicate this summer to a season of healing. I have thought about this for a while. I really believe that each of us is here to learn and explore largely by relationships. We might even be patching up mistakes from other lives we have lived. I take this idea very seriously. Each day I ask for guidance, so I may accomplish in this life exactly what I intended during this incarnation. This is what has me committed to cleaning up my mistakes. I want to find peace with some of my past actions. I'm pressing the redo button. I'm reaching out to some of the people in my past where I was hurt, or I hurt others. I'm giving myself the opportunity for closure. I want the freedom to know that I can face some of my fears and know that I'm still OK.

This summer I'm also blessed with my oldest daughter coming home for the summer. This has allowed me to recognize the importance of grabbing this time and making the most of it! I really want to take the time to let each family member feel loved and recognized. I want to make the most of the time we have together, to heal our little piece of the world. Yep, my family knows that this summer is all about sharing our feelings and letting things go.

As a busy mother of three there were many times that I felt like I was just putting out fires. I didn't have the time, or didn't take the time, for some of the issues at hand. Well, those issues are still waiting for my attention. It's kind of like sweeping something under the carpet. The dirt is still there. I'm going to do my best to really address my relationship with each person in our family… probably even the dogs!

In addition to communicating honestly, I'm going to try some alternative therapies. I think it's really fun to explore different healing techniques. I'm ready to make a shift to feeling satisfaction with my entire life. That's a big deal! I'm ready to let go of the blame I have for myself and others. I know as I get in touch with my fears I will be one step closer to a life of unconditional love.

I share pieces of my personal journey and I hope that can I inspire others to join me during this time of healing. If any of my stories or messages resonate with you, let me know. As always, I'm sending prayers that we all connect in the most compassionate way with unconditional love guiding us.

Channeled message

The idea of healing or the process of healing is simply a way of letting go of what has weighed you down. It is when you realize you to are free to choose any path. All paths and all choices are open to you. You have always been loved and will always be loved. We will sit by and watch you discover your divine self. When you're ready, and only when you're ready, we will ask you to join us on the other side where you will also discover the beauty of the journey.

Earth is a magnificent force of energy. Some people are able to find their way, their connection while experiencing life on Earth. That's the goal. Remember, we are always here for each spiritual being. We are here for each other. The greatest gift you have is one another. It's through the ability to experience grief and compassion and undeniable love that we all find our true self, our divine self. So, shed your fears, ask for guidance and trust that we're always near. Trust the connection to self and source.

Divine guidance to the center of wellness and peace is here at every moment for you. Reconnect with the energy that brought you to this vital moment that explains the very nature of you. Courageous and loving, you are a network of divine interventions and miracles. the rest falls away. your highest self that consists of only love and joy is what we always recognize in you. It's what we are designed to recognize in all. Together we will form the circle of divinity.

End channeling

Andrea Reiman- Unsp

Expanding through Karma

I LOVE THE POWER of the Law of Attraction. I will even go so far as to call it a lifestyle. The premise is easy to grasp. Thinking good thoughts = feeling good = good life. I agree with this. However, I also think we come into this world with life lessons to master. Some might call these life lessons Karma. Others believe these lessons are what God created just for you. Many believe we created these lessons before our current incarnation, to help us evolve.

Life lessons, or karma, have the end result of impacting humanity in a beautiful way. Both help you connect with your tribe or soul group and together you raise the global vibration. You and your tribe bring an element of awareness to our world. This also increases our personal ability to manifest and attract love and peace in our world.

There are several things that we can learn in our human lives. One is, don't take everything so personally. By this I mean there is an art to observing and not reacting to each situation in our life. Don't allow yourself to be lost in the event. We also need to connect with forgiveness. When we can be objective and even find forgiveness in life situations, we can reach out and help others.

When I was in my late teens my older brother committed suicide with a gun. I still feel grief and sadness for his time on earth. He suffered mental illness and experienced a very tragic life. This loss helped me recognize the pain that many people experience through their entire lives. It helped bring awareness into my heart. This was a stepping stone in knowing that there is so much more than our human life. I remember being so sad, without the words to explain my emptiness. I still feel a sadness for my brother's pain, but I have made peace with the loss. His death helped me gain an understanding of eternity.

About ten years following my brother's death I had another significant experience.

I was going out for a hike with a good friend. It was a full moon and a beautiful night. We got a late start, which I remember caused me great frustration. When we pulled into the parking lot, there was one car leaving. There was only one truck left in the dark parking lot. My friend and I didn't make it very far down the trail before we encountered victims of a shooting.

Without going into detail about the event, my eyes were once again opened to something so much greater than our human lives. The person who did the shootings was on a mission to see what it felt like to kill someone. If we had arrived at my desired time, my friend and I might have been victims as well.

I spent hours applying pressure to the gunshot wounds of one of the victims. My friend tried to get help. One person survived. One person died. The time I spent in the darkness with the victims, felt tied to a past life. Many years later I visited the state where the shooting took place. It happened to be the exact weekend that an article was published by the young women that survived. In the writing she referenced me and wondered how the shooting had affected my life.

The tragedy brought a sense of awareness and even awe for the connection we share with each other in this life and beyond. My heart was opened again to the magical orchestrations that occur for perfect timing of encounters.

I have lingering effects from the night of the shootings. I still have sadness for my brother. But greater than the fear and the loss is my connection to peace. I believe that is part of why I'm here; I help others find an awareness of peace. My soul group is growing day by day. Our vibration is peace.

When we are aware of how the Law of Attraction works, our life unfolds beautifully. Just as important as Law of Attraction is Karma. Life lessons bring expansion. Together we live in a time of great expansion. Together we expand.

Channeled message

The shift to awareness that has begun is powerful. You're releasing many things from the past, both individually and collectively. Don't be afraid of the pain or grief. There is a new energy to help you release everything that is not vibrating light. Guidance for releasing grief is always near you. Just ask. You have been given the strength and awareness to fully experience a world in the emerging light. Release anything that binds you to fear. Release yourself of any burdens of mankind thought. Celebrate the joy that replenishes your world, body and soul.

This is truly a time of immense discovery and passion. Just as strong as the energy that is shaking the world free of binding thoughts is the miracle of love, light and joy that is sweeping things clean and filling us up. Our thoughts are more powerful now than ever. Ask for help in releasing what is not yours. Ask for help in finding your place in the new world. Your brilliance is totally shining in all complete power and light. I stand in awe.

End of channel

In this channel I was shown that everything that is surfacing now is part of a cleansing. Think of all the revelations in the news regarding past acts. We release energy and make way for new energy. I was shown huge waves and currents of this clearing energy. This can make things a little rough as they are released. I'm also shown how we have more help from Angels and guides than ever before!

Ask for assistance through this time. It's really exciting to watch our expansion!

We See through the Same Eyes

WE ARE A group of divine members selected to work with you. We have been with you, around you and within you from the conception of time, or in other words, forever. You cannot separate yourself from our energy. We're the connection to all that is. We're only one form of this connection. There are many ways to connect to light energy, but at this moment we are your connection to all. Acknowledge your existence in this human form as well as spiritual form. We ask that you allow us to help you open up in a more available way to your source energy. Become more aware of your own divine energy and less aware of what distracts you from pure source, love and light.

Know that you are already free of judgment, free of pain and loss. Your only awareness is your purpose to love and explore love. Your joy escapes you and builds the connection between heaven and Earth. There are no mistakes about why you're here at this point with these lessons. Observe your ability to change everything with the simple appreciation of this moment.

We help you fully open up. We explain the design of your

intricately beautiful destination of the complete and expanded self. Let us guide you on this journey of remembering who you are and what you're made of. We laugh with you as you become more aware of your light and let go of the fragments of doubt that clouded the vision of your magnitude.

Your expansion is causing the higher vibration of light and love to change the currencies of energy on Earth. This also changes the polarization of Earth. Don't be alarmed by the swiftness that such changes occur. Once it begins, it creates an opening for expansion of self for all. The confusion will lessen . This process has already begun, and the telling signs of the shift are already at hand. We're already walking and talking as one as we merge with you and stand with you as you begin to see all, through our eyes.

To understand that our eyes see the same and are the same. We all experience the expansion as one. We will breathe as one, teach as one, and accept as one. The feeling of love and light expands and grows and creates a place of infinite pleasure and joy and freedom and greatness to stand in the awareness. The human body will not be needed and in fact cannot experience the intense realms of ascension or awareness or shift of this magnitude…

We gently release you back to Earth to share your stories of possibilities and love. We release you to continue your journey exploring and teaching on Earth. But know that we are part of you and will remain uninjured and in perfect formation through all your journey. We will continue to help you heal and understand your completeness, your magnificence. That has already taken place and only needs to be remembered. With loving guidance, your magnificent self.

End channel

We're given many interesting opportunities for living with awareness and achieving grace in our lives. Taking my lessons in my human life combined with the awareness I have received through channeling I believe we can experience great joy and abundance on Earth. We have the ability to create an amazing life for ourselves. I encourage us all to fully experience the joys of the physical, emotional and intellectual self.

Fully discover what your body can experience. Perhaps you will find limitations that you thought existed, are no longer there. Take care of your body. Nourish your body with clean fruits and vegetables. Drink clean water. Sleep. How does it feel to really care for the human body you have been given? How does it feel to use the human body you were given?

Challenge your mind. Learn about what intrigues you for the sake of learning. Share with others as you explore your interests. Share your interpretation of what you're learning. You may find your soul group as you explore your intellectual capacity. Your intellect can offer you direction in life. It's all about following what you're passionate about! This is a never-ending journey.

Our emotional selves are powerful! When we open our hearts and are willing to explore all the feelings that come in, our world changes. This is part of your intuitive self. Learning how to discern energy and love. The biggest step is loving yourself and knowing we're all one. We're all connected. We're all love. This is when communicating with words is no longer needed. We communicate as one, with our thoughts.

We are given these amazing bodies, minds and spirits to explore the universe with. Stay in touch with your guides and Angels. Trust and have faith as you give yourself permission to fully live and experience all that life has to offer. Be as courageous as you can, your magnificence is always part of you. When you and I are finally done with this experience I know that a world of beautiful images, wholeness and compassion is awaiting our full attention. It takes only a thought to conceive a miracle

I hope this finds you thriving in all you do. My world continues to be full of opportunities and funny little events that keep leading me onward. I'm happy to see the snow melting and the birds returning

to Alaska. I'm so grateful for all the people that are in my life. From the bottom of my heart I thank all those that connect with me for coaching, intuitive reading or just a laugh!

This is a great time to think about the people and animals in your life and what they mean to you. If you feel inspired let them know how much you appreciate them. Possibly some people have taught you some uncomfortable lessons. These are of value also. We're all in this together, whatever roles we play. This week I'm going to really be conscious of how others have contributed to my life. I encourage you to try this also.

I visualized the channeled message below as a symbol of eternity. We achieve awareness only to be rebirthed again and again until we can see ourselves fully connected to God, of God. We (soul groups) all work closely together to bring about the moment of self-realization and healing for all. Maybe the time has come for miracles to be our way of life and to recognize how close we are to our higher power. We only need to look deep inside.

Channeled message

Look closely into the eyes you examine your life through. Those eyes are who you are and what you see. Look deeper into those eyes and even deeper still and you will find the passage to uncovering the wisdom and blessings that have been shifting inside of you. They have been waiting for you to remember. You're so close to touching God and being aware of God in all your doings. Know that you never fell short of any one's expectations, unless it is your own.

Take hold of the footing on your internal path to wisdom that has been shining away inside of you

your entire world and purpose waits for you to remember. Your mind becomes clear, your words are faithful, your actions are of compassion. There is no afterthought, there is only the now. Take my hand and turn off the sound that surrounds you. Take my hand and I will steady you as we walk side by side deeper into the path that leads to truth and awareness. It's at this moment that your radiance can come forth. Your heart anticipates this moment of self-realization. You're more complete now than ever before.

As we continue down this path we realize how close we have existed with truth but have not experienced truth. We explore further down this passage of wisdom and observe the miracles that are just waiting to take form. It's your time to give life to the miracles. These miracles have been resting inside you. It's time to lose all beliefs except those of your true nature. We will continue deeper into this passage that is held so closely inside you. You have guarded and not trusted yourself with what is so perfectly formed with in you.

We continue down this path that begins to look familiar. It's the fertile ground of awareness and compassion. We travel deeper inside still and witness the connection that has taken place to create

this perfect image of you and I combined. This amazing passage contains a gift so glorious it can't be contained any longer. It's finally time for you to express yourself in miracles. Speak of miracles and live miracles.

We understand at first this is an awkward experience, coming from a place that serves only love, being born back into a place of confusion. We hold you dear and will help you gain the wisdom to share miracles in all you do.

We ask that you continue to trust and take our hand let us guide you back into the familiar place that you once stood without hesitation. This place of safety and love calls to you. You can stop the confusion at any time by reaching inside and remembering where you came from and how you began.

End of Channel

If we take one step to the left, or one step to the right, our path will be changed forever.

Alas we are exactly where we're supposed to be.

One of the greatest messages I get for 2018 is the importance of reconnecting with our life force energy. This can be felt strongly through our connection to Earth. We frequently view the Earth Energy as separate from Divine Energy. They are one and the same. Earth Energy is what is guiding us into the New Age and offers us one of the many portals that contains our collective wisdom and strength. We're being asked to seek a greater connection to the Divine through our Mother Earth.

Earth Energy contains the magnetic fields that interact with us each on an individual basis. We each contain unique cellular data (memories) that is triggered by Earth energies. This is the reason that some people are experiencing the great shift and others are not. Eventually all will be pulled into the flow of knowing.

It's our individual energetic and divine make-up that react to the higher frequency of the Earth's charges. This is why many of us will find ourselves in uncharted territories. This is the energy that will move us to find our higher self and connect to the plan of our greater good.

This may bring what appears as chaos into our World. It will bring unplanned for events into our life path. We will see much more geographic, weather, power, and water activity. The secret to maintaining peace in this experience is staying grounded and seeking guidance from our Earth and all our messengers. At all times we're guided, protected and enlightened. We only need to breathe, connect and allow.

Channeled message

I recognize the energy that moves the trees and rises through the air and settles on the ground. I recognize this energy as the endless source of abundance that connects us all. We are in the process of being called to find our strength, our knowingness and our character and purpose. Our connection to the Divine resides in all we say and do.

We absorb the wisdom of the trees, sky and water through our eyes, and all our senses. The Earth energy resides within you at this moment, connecting you to all times on Earth and beyond.

Earth is much greater than can be imagined. It contains our collective heart energy. It contains the past and the future and all that is.

As our energetic poles shift and allow new vibrations, we find ourselves experiencing new gifts of sight, sound and creation. This is the experience of feeling and knowing and allowing our greater self to emerge.

The energy of the Earth pulsates through us all, carries Divine messages for all and heals us all.

This moment in time has never been so strong, so powerful. The pull we feel is guiding us into the new era. Yes, new pathways are being discovered. New ways of communication will become available. New ways of understanding time and our conscious availability. (Our concept of consciousness will evolve.) New ways of understanding neuro transmitters and how energy works with in and around our bodies and how we really are affected by gravity, the moon, and tides and how the tides will subtly shift as our awareness grows to encompass our spiritual self and our individual and collective spiritual unfolding.

Behold the greatness in the moment of self- discovery.

Behold the greatness of allowing yourself to truly explore the depths of compassion, peace and the reminder of why we have all come together to orchestrate the greatest collision of beauty, peace, love, light and intelligence. There is such timeless beauty to what has been created for our Divine experience. Intricate webs of inspiration have manifested such perfection that lays deep within us all. I see miracles upon miracles unfolding in and around us all.

Divine expression of humanity is unfolding in our collective consciousness.

We are realizing the truth together.

I am connected to the Earth,

The almighty powers of the Earth

And all that is

It is time for the Earth to start speaking

It is time for us to start listening

End of channel

I'm excited for each of us to experience a deeper knowing. Let's stick together and share our experiences as our world offers exciting new ways to bond and support each other.

For me personally, my writing and channeled messages will be shared on a greater level. I'm excited for an amazing year of growth!

Here are a few predictions:

- We will see much more earthquake activity etc. We will experience some big black outs in our country on both coasts.

- Our seas will experience new patterns of travel. This will be both in new water currents as well as conflicts at sea.

- We will also experience conflicts in air travel. It has more to do with the way information is being shared. It almost feels like there will be a group that holds hostage or takes data /or the way data is processed. This will affect travel and the way our money is processed.

- By 2019 we will have the beginnings of different channels for communication. This is related to what is occurring now in 2018. Our channels for finances and air travel and security will develop new strategies. It almost feels like flight pattern info just vanishes into thin air. Like there is a void where a plan once was.

- Watch for some activity in the area of Greece. Watch Belgium as well. These are separate events.

Use this information as an opportunity to observe. The big picture is that we're right where we're supposed to be. We all have the ability to experience the deepest meaning of love and light.

Healing from The Inside Out

RECENTLY I SCHEDULED a little retreat for myself at a resort in Arizona. As soon as I arrived I was transported into the land of healing. All my spiritual, emotional and physical needs could be addressed. Healthy food, energy work and nice accommodations were at my fingertips. I had so many choices of activities, yoga, guided meditation, rock climbing and amazing spa options.

Miraval Resort offers something for everyone. A handful of guests visit to process grief. Others are on the quest to find their life purpose or just simply take a break from a demanding life. Yet there is an overall resounding theme of most guests. They are seeking healing from some pain in their life. I personally came for unscheduled time and inspiration. I wanted to explore different healing modalities… Plus, I always meet amazing people at pivotal times in their lives when traveling.

What struck me most on this stay was the variety of conscious shifting that was taking place. We all have different needs for healing and our ailments come in all different forms. We each treat our bodies and minds differently even with the simple cold. Occasionally we also need to care for our bodies during more serious Dis Ease (disease). We each process grief differently. We each move through hurt and illness differently. We all have vastly different tools available to us. I know there is one type of healing that we can all benefit from. Healing from the inside out.

Let's first explore how dis ease manifests in our life. I believe that many of our illness start on an energetic level. This means that it affects our energy body (energy surrounding our human body), much sooner than it does in our physical body. Our physical bodies are surrounded by and filled with Divine energy. We also have the ebb and flow of the energy that we attract. Each of us, also has our individual energy that we are born with. So, we have a mixture of divine energy, personal energy (karma for this life) and the energy we attract by our thoughts and behaviors. The Karmic energy can bring various opportunities into our energy field.

Imagine a new born baby born with this beautiful, light energy field. Divine energy is abundant, and the karmic energy is there as well. At this stage the baby is learning how to interact with the world. For the most part living in the moment. As the older the baby grows, it has expectations and law of attraction begins to come into play. This baby learns that what it thinks about triggers behaviors that result in the desired outcome. All is good, there is a nice flow of energy between the baby and the universe. Just like the baby, we are constantly connected to the energy of the Universe. It flows to us, surrounds us and hopefully easily flows through us. This is the abundance of life.

As our journey of life continues we can start acquiring blocks in our flow of energy. This can be in the form of disappointment, lack of self-care and being around people that are not treating us well. As these blocks in our energy field grow they decrease the flow of energy. The ability to live in the moment and welcome a life of abundance decreases.

This negative energy that has taken residence in the person's energy field is denser than the original vibrant energy. It's heavier and can weigh your heart and mind down. The longer it stays in your field, the deeper it takes root. it will eventually begin to settle into the physical body. Up until this point the symptoms are found more in our mind. We might have recognized being emotionally tired, depressed and attracting unwanted things into our lives. It's also at this point that some people turn to self- medication or even co-dependent relationships. If drugs and alcohol are brought into the balance, it's even more toxic.

As the dense energy settles into the body we start experiencing physical symptoms. We might experience weight changes, fatigue or aches and pains. It can trigger auto immune disease and other serious issues. At a certain point many of us seek medical attention. This can be standard Western care or even non -traditional therapies. They all have a place in the process of healing. Some are more loving then others. For example, having surgery can be very hard on your body, as is taking medication with harsh side effects. If you think about it, we willingly do some pretty painful things in the name of good health.

If you're seeking a life of ease and abundance and good health. How do you get rid of the murky unwanted energy stored up from every break up, negative self- talk and poor self -care?

First off clean up your environment. If you're intertwined with a job or relationship that is unkind to you, take steps to let them go. Your health is not worth sacrificing for a job. When you are living a life of abundance, the perfect job will come to you. Are you treating your body with love? Do you regularly eat healthy fruits and veggies? Are fruits and vegetables your staple? Are you sleeping enough? Do you enjoy fresh water and air? Are you enjoying physical activity? Do you get time outside in nature? Do you have a supportive community? These are all fundamental for good health.

The most important aspect of good health is regular prayer and meditation. This is healing from the inside out. Call in that beautiful Divine Energy into your body through prayer and meditation. The more you do this, the easier it is to let go of all the pains from the past, clearing your energy. See your -self as healed and perfect in every sense. Treat yourself like you are a miracle, because you are.

Ask God, the Universe and Angels to heal you and remove anything that is not for your highest good. Provide yourself with love and enjoy the abundance that flows to you and trough you. Live with gratitude for all the opportunities bestowed upon you in this life. Know that you're no less a miracle than anything else. As you dive deeper into this place of abundance and gratitude you will find your disease slipping farther and farther away. There will be no scars left from the dense energy. only gratitude for the lessons learned while discovering self-love. Let the healing begin.

Touching Clarity

I AM BLESSED WITH a rewarding and busy life. This includes being a parent, wife, and business owner. My intuitive work and channeling have gifted me with the experience of connection to other realities. My world has changed because of this. Sometimes it feels like I can reach out and touch another place that is filled with so much love and compassion it makes me cry. In truth I can reach there, in my mind. So how do these two worlds merge?

Is it possible to move from a place with so much uncertainty to a place of absolute compassion and awareness, using only your consciousness of self? Is it possible to be aware of the endless peace of one world and exist in another world of conflict? Can I dance in between these worlds?

Compassion, love and awareness are our birthright. These are what we as individuals come here to understand. Can we each learn about love, compassion and awareness while living such vastly different lives? I know we can. I believe we came here to gain insight from all our potential experiences. We're here to establish that fear is the only thing that can derail us from our purpose of love and creativity.

We have mistakenly placed confidence in a world outside of our own thoughts and our personal connection to the Universe. We have created a world that believes there is something greater than the power of our mind and the universe. You see everything really does start and end in its complete form in this thought, right now. I see it as we each have an unlimited amount of possibilities or thoughts to choose from. They are all available right now in this instant. This mystical journey begins with each of us realizing we design our lives with our mind and thoughts.

The thought process is built in your mind as a switchboard or receiver of infinite possibilities. You are connected to the Universe and Eternity by your thought. But there is more to the thought process then people realize. It holds your greatest gifts of connection to creative energy and potential for love. The reason you have individual thoughts and abilities to pull into other energy fields is to share this expansive energy process. Imagine each thought that we allow ourselves to dive into has the imprint of our individual soul. Our thoughts can carry the eternal messages of love from our soul. This is part of our creative intelligence. This is our message of love.

It's possible to be aware of the power of our mind and thrive in this Earth-bound world... yes. Your mind can take you to amazing places of endless love and compassion. Your thoughts can open a line of communication with others that will change your perspective of this world.

How do you want to view and experience the world? If you

could paint all the details of the world and your life experiences what would it look like? If you had the power to take away or add to your life what would it look like? The trick here is keep an open mind. Don't allow yourself to come up with why it won't work. Design your unique life with an open heart and mind. What are you truly longing for? It could be simply the connection to eternal love and compassion.

We are learning to share what is the most important feature of all, love. Love has always been the guiding force and always will be. The strongest currents of love are found where compassion and creativity are shared. where minds come together and share the vision of peace and unity. It's here where expansion takes place. This expansion is not just in our mind. it allows your soul to expand and shift and share the complete awareness and connection to all… It allows the beauty of all lifeforms, all energetic exchanges to take place at once. It allows the breath to settle into each cell of the physical body and allow transformation to take place. a complete awareness of self and how you fit so perfectly into this world that was created by you…

Our souls are working together to create the perfect blend of energies that will capture our awareness and bring us into the new paradigm shift. Rest assured that all souls are taking part in this shift. We all agreed to play a role that would transform the energy into heart felt awareness… You need do nothing more than be aware of the kindness and compassion that is a part of your make up. Allow your genuine strength and compassion to flow into all your thoughts and actions. Imagine your unique thought patterns joining all the other beautiful example of creative compassion. Imagine this new discovery guiding you towards your perfect world where you're supported by love and compassion always. In closing, enjoy this moment of living in a time of two worlds merging.

The flow of light unto your soul is deep and rich. The human form is mixed with much stronger and greater forces that come alive when you recognize you are the flow of life. We're asking you to awaken your soul with memories deep in your past imbedded deep in your thoughts, your actions even your DNA. People speculate on the DNA molecules. Yes, your DNA holds the answers to your cells, but also to your deep-seated fears, and love. We can help you release your fears with the knowledge that time has stopped. There is nothing more to move forward to. It has already happened. If you take your dreams and uncover the fear that is holding them hostage, you will find the brightness of your future. It's already here. Just waiting to be remembered and celebrated in deep sense of gratitude.

Angels and guides want you to hear and understand that you have already achieved your greatness… There is nothing more to prove. Nothing more to want. Imagine your heart opening and sharing all of God's creation. No exception. This is for you to explore. It is what you make of it. It's your inheritance. Imagine taking out one fragment at a time, (fragments of creation) and discovering the beauty each holds. This is where you are. Exploring one life event at a time. With expansion and greater awareness, you will experience all that is, as one. All possibilities are controlled by you. How does it feel to explore more than one option of life? We ask you to examine your role in creation. What are you creating with your unlimited potential?

You're expanding at a greater speed now. Soon you will recognize your power to speak with others with no words (think even other species). You will hear new sounds. You will remember the skills required to adjust to the light and energy around you and within you... New frequencies are running deep and changing everything on a cellular level. We will start to see babies with new characteristics... Those on planet Earth will begin to experience new sensations and even adapt to the changing energy. Do not fear the rapid changes. Know that we are right here with you and this truly is the time of great shift to remembering.

Ask for guidance. Trust your feet and hands, Trust what you feel and hear. New languages will be taught in school. Our ability to merge with others is increasing at a rapid rate. It's a time of emergence. And acceptance... New stories blend with old, the ancient tongues become fresh again. We lead you into safe spaces...

Don't recognize the fear or misplaced energy that is sometimes available. It's nothing more than an absence of light. We call in the light to surround you in all ways, at all moments. You are made of light. Gratitude for adhering to our plan of great expansion. You're expanding in light and love. Guided by peace and compassion, you are always recognized as the beautiful light that resides in your soul.

Spiritual Wellness

I have been back home in Alaska for about a week now. I was in California enjoying hiking and a half marathon. I was also there to bring our oldest home from her first year of college.

It became apparent sometime during the year that living in the middle of all a city was not a good fit for her emotionally. Even though there was the beautiful sun that she craved, the constant chaos was too much. She has decided to transfer schools.

The challenges of the school year brought some gifts as well. She came home with clarity on what she needs in her life. Does she know how it will all come together? No. But she clearly knows what she needs and what she can't tolerate.

As a parent, it is very difficult to see your child, or any loved one, experience some tough lessons. I was experiencing my own lessons through the year. This struggle is what inspired me to focus on healing. We all are exposed to challenges. How we react and what take away from them are key.

This summer our daughter is home learning how to nurture herself. This by itself is a valuable lesson. As is finding a physical place where you feel safe. When you experience safety and support, you can process what is going on in your life. This rejuvenates you, so you have the energy carry on.

Finding a safe spiritual space is just as important. My safe spiritual place was founded in prayer and meditation. Eventually it progressed to me having conversations with God and my Angels and Guides on a regular basis. Because I have created this relationship between myself and my Spiritual team, I know home is always near. Much like falling into a loved one's arms, I fall into my Spiritual safe spot.

I encourage you to attempt two things in the next two weeks. First, create a space where you feel safe. The simpler the better. Make it your own with essential oils, candles, crystals… Anything that is healing to you. Pets are also great to invite into your safe healing space.

The next is check into your spiritual space. Are you taking care of the relationships within this sacred space? Are you using this healing energy on a regular basis? A good indicator of your spiritual space is knowing where your level faith is. Do you know that everything is OK? Do you recognize you are never alone? Spend time pondering these questions. Your spiritual space is with you wherever you are. It's always ready and available to provide comfort.

As most of you know, I share a lot about myself and my life. I hope this allows people to connect with my ideas and lessons.

I love getting the feedback! If you want ideas on creating safe spaces, contact me through my website.

Abundance and Everything

PEOPLE WANT TO know how to live a life of abundance. They also want to increase their intuitive skills. How do I know this? I'm asked about these, more than any other question. So how can we all live an intuitive and abundant life?

The most important thing to understand is they are not separate. If you're living an intuitive life, you're living an abundant life. They are one in the same. Both are manifested through realizing our connection with source. When we recognize we're all connected to the same web of energy; abundance is manifested. We can call this Law of Attraction, living in the flow or living in the moment. It's really just remembering that you are a part of an eternal energy.

The next step is to come up with your idea of abundance. If you have created a life that includes wealth and prosperity and yet you're still afraid of lack or poverty, you're not in the flow. An individual that lives a life knowing their needs are always met is experiencing abundance. The trick is remembering sometimes you need to let go and trust. We might not know how or when, but we must have faith in our abundance.

How does it feel to experience the zone or in the moment?

I'll share one of my mornings a few days ago. I had just finished meditating. One of our dogs was resting next to me. I heard my son come up stairs to start his day. As soon our dog heard Finn, he left my side and greeted my son. My son hugged Ringo and they sat next to each other by the fire. They enjoyed a moment of unconditional love. Nothing cluttered the moment. Because they were both able to put their worries aside and just experience love, they were attracting more ease and love. They both intuitively have trust in their eternal bond.

Another step to creating an abundant life is recognizing where you feel good. When we take the time to honor our feelings, we're getting closer to living in the zone. If you don't feel good around certain people, decrease your time with them. If you feel like you're wasting your time at a crappy job, you are. Creating an environment that supports you physically, mentally and emotionally is crucial for staying in the moment. In the beginning as you create your ideal life, you may only have moments of feeling connected to our higher power. As your moments increase, you gain more faith and experience abundance. Think of it as part of a giant magnet. Once you start feeling good, you attract more feel-good moments.

I have mentioned the word recognize several times so far. This is important. We must each individually do our part to create a life that feels good. This means we need to pay attention to how we feel. We need to call in more feel good moments. We need to have courage to take the next step in creating our personal idea of abundance. It might not look like anybody else's abundant life. Remember abundance is not just a personal lifestyle, it is a feeling.

So how does intuition fit into this? One of the things that happens when you feel good, you let your barriers down. You're not worried about things. You are open to receiving. The main component of intuition is being able to receive. This is why it's so important to be able to connect to the feel-good moments and be open to receiving. The less stress we experience the more our abundance and intuitive channels are wide open for receiving.

With practice you will be able to go to that feel-good place and connect at almost any time. This is because the place is inside you. So where ever you are, that intuitive, abundant place can be found.

Channeled message

A newness awaits you in this cycle of exchanging energy. The moment at hand is bringing you to awareness that you're free from your past and free from the future. You can tune into your internal guidance and take part in the cosmic intelligence. This reality rests in each of us. In all beings the universal spark of awareness lights the way to a place where consciousness has evolved to oneness, one time, one place, one being. We're all evolving as one. There is an awareness that sees the unlimited capacity of our potential. We are there. In the same way that we're all experiencing confusion and healing and war. It's how we understand energy and intention that pulls us to cosmic intelligence.

It is the idea of time that has created fragile minds. Within us all is everything free of time, free of space, free of boundaries. It's this eternal light that connects us all.

End of Channel

During this channel I was shown how we (humans) are fighting against time. Our cosmic awareness doesn't operate with the awareness of time. Our human selves have built a world around the concept of time. And so, the confusion begins. I believe that this one concept is what brings many people to a place of feeling confused and ungrounded. So the more you meditate, enjoy nature and animals, the better you feel.

Another concept I was shown involve specific connections. The words consciousness, moment, source, (and many others) all can be exchanged. When we really connect to the moment we connect to the internal light, source, all that is, etc.

Enjoy The Moment

I'M BLESSED WITH a very rewarding and busy life. This includes being a parent, wife, and business owner. My intuitive work and channeling have gifted me with the experience of connection to other realities. My world has changed because of this. Sometimes it feels like I can reach out and touch another place that is filled with so much love and compassion it makes me cry. In truth I can reach there, in my mind. So how do these two worlds merge?

Is it possible to move from a place with so much uncertainty to a place of absolute compassion and awareness; using only your consciousness of self? Is it possible to be aware of the endless peace of one world and exist in another world of conflict? Can I dance in between these worlds?

Compassion, love and awareness are our birth right. These are what we as individuals come here to understand. Can we each learn of love, compassion and awareness while living such vastly different lives? I know we can. I believe we came here to gain insight from all our potential experiences. We're here to establish that fear is the only thing that can derail us from our purpose of love and creativity.

We have mistakenly placed confidence in a world outside of our own thoughts and our personal connection to the Universe. We have created a world that believes there is something greater than the power of our mind and the universe. You see everything really does start and end in its complete form in this thought, right now. I see it as we each have an unlimited amount of possibilities or thoughts to choose from. They are all available right now in this instant. This mystical journey begins with each of us realizing we design our lives with our mind and thoughts.

The thought process is built in your mind as a switchboard or receiver of infinite possibilities. You're connected to the Universe and Eternity by your thought. But there is more to the thought process then people realize... it holds your greatest gifts of connection to creative energy and potential for love. The reason you have individual thoughts and abilities to pull into other energy fields is to share this expansive energy process. Imagine each thought that we allow ourselves to dive into, has the imprint of our individual soul. Our thoughts can carry the eternal messages of love from our soul. This is part of our creative intelligence. This is our message of love.

It is possible to be aware of the power of our mind and thrive in this Earth-bound world? Yes. Your mind can take you to amazing places of endless love and compassion. Your thoughts can open a line of communication with others that will change your perspective of this world...

How do you want to view and experience the world? If you

could paint all the details of the world and your life experiences what would it look like? If you had the power to take away or add to your life what would it look like? The trick here is keep an open mind... don't allow yourself to come up with why it won't work. Design your unique life with an open heart and mind. What are you truly longing for? It could be simply the connection to eternal love and compassion.

We're learning to share what is the most important feature of all, love. Love has always been the guiding force and always will be. The strongest currents of love are found where compassion and creativity are shared, where minds come together and share the vision of peace and unity. It's here where expansion takes place. This expansion is not just in our mind. It allows your soul to expand and shift and share the complete awareness and connection to all... It allows the beauty of all life forms, all energetic exchanges to take place at once. It allows the breath to settle into each cell of the physical body and allow transformation to take place. a complete awareness of self and how you fit so perfectly into this world that was created by you.

Our souls are working together to create the perfect blend of energies that will capture our awareness and bring us into the new paradigm shift. Rest assured that all souls are taking part in this shift. We all agreed to play a role that would transform the energy into heart felt awareness...

You need do nothing more than be aware of the kindness and compassion that is a part of your make up. Allow your genuine strength and compassion to flow into all your thoughts and actions. Imagine your unique thought patterns joining all the other beautiful example of creative compassion. Imagine this new discovery guiding you towards your perfect world where you're supported by love and compassion always.

In closing, enjoy this moment when you live in a time of two worlds merging.

Shahastra - Meeting the Self Reflection Cards

The Brilliance of Love

Months ago, I decided to put my focus on healing. This healing was not just for myself, but for my family and humanity at large. We are now firmly planted on the path towards complete healing of mind, body and soul; but we must connect deeper unto the awareness of love.

Stay with me as I prioritize love in my life and share what happens in my blogs.

I recently became aware of the many people that I care about who are seeking the perfect life partner. They are seeking love. This of course caused me to stop and look at the love in my life. And so, I find myself wanting to dive in deeper and be much more committed to experiencing love in a deeper way.

I am making the commitment not just for myself, or my family, but to all of humanity and the Universe to love deeper.

So here I am experiencing a feeling of vulnerability and excitement. As I explore how to open my heart even more to love, I have the faith and courage to do so. I believe that part of the reason I'm here on Earth is to help others make sense of our promise to carry forth our unique rays of love, light and peace on Earth. To make this happen I feel committed to share my understanding of love through my life experiences. And so, I share my personal experiences, hoping it helps others find the courage to commit to love. I want us not just to commit to love, but to explore love and share love and live love, with no boundaries.

One important aspect to recognize that we are made of love, even more then flesh and bone. You see the love came before the physical self. The love is woven into each cell and each thought. We only have to shift our minds to recognize this. When we do shift our minds to recognize love, the void between you and me becomes smaller. Imagine all of humanity pulsating with the vibration of love. This is where we are headed.

Some of our experiences on Earth have caused us to lesson our awareness to the love that is so much a part of who we are. We have learned to monitor how and when we want to acknowledge love.

Think about how easy it is to have an open heart around your pets and young children. We are able to just recognize them for the love they are. All is right with the world. When we interact with a more mature person, we have expectations. It is at that point that we step back and start shutting down the open heart.

One skill needed to really stay open to the rays of love is releasing expectations. This I admit can be very challenging.

We are brought up in a society that teaches us to have expectations. We are taught to think in a very linear way. We are not encouraged to think outside the box. We not only have expectations of others, but of ourselves and society.

Our expectations is to contribute to a vision of the world that doesn't allow our light to shine as brilliant as it truly is. So, practice looking at yourself and others as a complete, perfect form of light. No judgement. Just hold the space of knowing that you and all you see is made of light. Start recognizing the love all around you.

Sometimes you need to take a breath and walk away from a situation. Imagine holding love and light all around the person or situation you needed a break from. It is so important to remember that you deserve to be treated with respect and love. It is always ok, and even necessary, to walk away from situations that hurt you or your loved ones. No reaction needed other than removing yourself from the pain. You have the ability to feel good and to feel bad. This is a tool. Choose what allows the flow of love and light into your life. The feel-good choice might not fit into our linear thinking, but go for it anyway!

Insulate yourself in love. The truth is you are already insulated in love, but I want you to remember how much love you have around you. The very fact that you have love woven into every part of you guarantees that you have attracted love to surround you. You only need to recognize it. So, between now and my next blog, place yourself in situations that let you feel good. This might be getting a massage, spending time with friends or walking barefoot outside. Whatever it takes to get you to a place of open heart, go for it.

Channeled message

Beginning from the dawn of time, you have been brilliantly lit with the light of love. It is just at this moment that you are able to view your true nature with fresh eyes and see the light burning brightly, radiating from your soul, feel and experience the youthful, radiant energy that has no sense of time, space, age, and know that you in fact come with a clean slate, a clear conscious.

A mind that fully functions with the power of love and light guiding you to harmonious experiences.

Flights of harmony, episodes of harmony, will blend into one, as that is your true nature.

The shift to silence the fear has begun and is well under way.

We salute you in your ability to find the path that is true. The next phase and how it is revealed will come as a shock to some. Some of you never believed in your ability to find true love and experience peace in this life form. I assure you, we assure you, that fear is the farthest from the truth.

We come as symbols of love, beacons of love. Look for the ways love shows up in your life.

Celebrate.

You will see bridges forming where there were none. You will discover now, openings within your own mind. People will begin to travel in a way never thought possible. Nature will be expanding and guiding those ready for the fullest expression of love and light.

For nature to expand, one must hold in their heart the availability of connecting to frequencies found in natural settings, a natural sequence of events. We are so excited to see the beginning is drawing near. The unraveling has begun and what is left will reveal the true nature of all. Behold your majestic nature – love, light and true peace.

End of channel

What this channel showed me is a symbol of eternity. But we finally have the vision to understand eternity. I'm also thinking that we will have some pretty amazing and powerful things that happen on Earth due to Mother Nature. The mention of bridges makes me think of our expanding consciousness and ability to communicate and travel in new ways. It takes this process of discovering our true nature to really experience love in totality.

In closing I am wishing everyone the brightest light shining on you. Thank you so much to everyone who reads my blog. Deepest gratitude for those that share how the messages relate to them. We are all part of this amazing transition to pure light...

Many, Many Blessings, Polly

www.ingramcontent.com/pod-product-compliance
Lightning Source LLC
LaVergne TN
LVHW072022060526
838200LV00058B/4647